SEEING THE FUTURE
 a beginner's guide

W0009006

LEILA BRIGHT

Hodder & Stoughton
A MEMBER OF THE HODDER HEADLINE GROUP

Acknowledgements

With thanks to Lucy Purkis, Sue Hart and Linda Miles

Order queries: please contact Bookpoint Ltd, 39 Milton Park, Abingdon, Oxon OX14 4TD. Telephone: (44) 01235 400414, Fax: (44) 01235 400454. Lines are open from 9.00–6.00, Monday to Saturday, with a 24 hour message answering service. Email address: orders@bookpoint.co.uk

British Library Cataloguing in Publication Data
A catalogue record for this title is available from The British Library

ISBN 0 340 73061 7

First published 1999
Impression number 10 9 8 7 6 5 4 3 2 1
Year   2003 2002 2001 2000 1999

Typeset by Transet Limited, Coventry, England.
Printed in Great Britain for Hodder & Stoughton Educational, a division of Hodder Headline Plc, 338 Euston Road, London NW1 3BH by Cox & Wyman Ltd, Reading, Berks.

CONTENTS

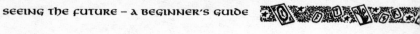

INTRODUCTION

I dwell in possibility
Emily Dickinson

Do you want to *change* your future? If so, it would help if you could *learn* something about that future. To predict is to foretell, or to prophesy, and the ancient arts of prediction described in this book can, at the very least, help you think about your future in new and challenging ways – they can help you learn. Whatever the basis of the methods discussed, they all have the same aim: to help you improve your life now and in the future, in whatever sphere particularly concerns you, whether that be relationships and sexuality, career and money, family life, health or education.

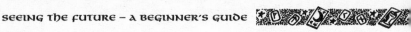

But can we really tell the future? And what might that mean? There are many well-documented cases of premonition, (forewarning of some event), clairvoyance (the faculty of seeing mentally what is happening or exists out of sight) and precognition (foreknowledge by unexplained means). But collectively, what do these cases amount to?

Before answering this question, it is important to be aware from the outset that none of the prophetic arts, not a single prophetic insight, deals in certainty. They all deal in probability, or in likelihood. Premonition, clairvoyance, precognition and the techniques for promoting them all tell us that something is more or less likely to happen, not that it will or will not happen.

None of the methods of prediction discussed yield information on some unmovable fate or destiny, but offer hints, warnings and suggestions about various paths open to you at a given time and point in your life. It is important to remember that you cannot abdicate responsibility for your own actions, or your own future, by experimenting with these methods. We all dwell in possibility, not certainty, whether we welcome its joys and terrors, or not.

Modern attitudes to prediction and oracles

In the West today, many people tend to be hostile to prediction. There is a variety of reasons for this. People think that:

- it is simply impossible to tell the future, time is constructed in such a way that prophecy is just not possible – hence all accounts to the contrary are the result of delusions, or are fraudulent; we might call this the sceptical objection;
- experimenting with prediction undermines our free will and responsibility – the moral objection;
- in trying to predict the future, humans are at the very least overreaching themselves, since knowledge of the future is and should be something reserved only for God – the religious objection;
- dishonest practitioners can and do mislead vulnerable people who come to them for advice – the practical objection.

If we are interested in prediction, we need to take these objections seriously. I have already touched on the moral objection, and suggested that an interest in exploring ancient arts does not imply a belief in fate, nor undermine our responsibility for ourselves or our actions. What about the other three objections?

We are entitled to ask the sceptics what they mean when they say that the nature of time makes foretelling the future impossible. What is the nature of time? In the West, we tend to think it moves forwards, like a straight arrow, only. But perhaps it can move backwards? Or turns in a wheel? Or forms a spiral? We can certainly imagine time travel, as the *Doctor Who* stories, and many others, illustrate. Telling each other stories about the future involves a kind of prediction. What has the sceptic to say about this? Finally, why is the sceptic so confident that all accounts of prophecy and similar phenomena must be delusional or fraudulent? In our society we tend to undervalue testimony, but why?

Religious arguments are well beyond the scope of this book, but it is worth pointing out that in the East, where ideas about Karma – a kind of web of responsibility spread over time – and reincarnation are commonplace elements of religious life, attitudes to the possibility that past, present and future might interweave in the life of one individual are far more relaxed than they are in the West.

To circumvent the scenario raised by the practical objection, in this book it is assumed that you, the reader, will be most interested in using these arts *yourself*, to investigate your *own* future, so the possibility of malicious deception by another cannot arise – the only person you can deceive is yourself. You should not attempt to use these arts to advise other people, without first undertaking a great deal more study and training. If you decide to consult a professional astrologer, tarot reader (or whatever) try to find somebody through word of mouth, as personal recommendation is one sign of reliability. Ask if your chosen practitioner is a member of any recognised organisation or body, and check that he or she has a reasonable and comprehensible scale of fees.

Despite the West's relatively hostile attitude to ancient arts of prediction, more modern methods of foretelling possibilities are widely used and promoted. For example:

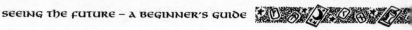

- Governments spend millions developing complicated computer models to predict: patterns of climate change; patterns of employment; the impact of disease or health screening programmes, etc. Indeed, it is probably fair to say that much of the work of government would grind to a halt if all its predictive functions were removed.
- Businesses spend millions trying to predict economic cycles – economic forecasting is a whole industry. Again, these predictions are mostly generated by computer.
- Advertisers and marketing agencies invest millions in trying to predict the next trend, fad, fashion or fancy. They do this solely so that they can try to sell us things we probably neither want nor need.
- Political parties invest huge amounts of money in databases to help them predict how the electorate will behave at election time.
- Millions of people gamble – on lotteries, on horses, on football, etc. Gambling is prediction in one of its simplest forms – I predict these numbers will come up on the lottery this week, or the dice will fall this way, or the red team will beat the blue team.

The modern methods of prediction used by governments, political parties, big business and the advertising industry all deal in probability – which is precisely what the ancient methods deal in, too. Most of the modern methods require expensive equipment and the backing of large organisations if they are to be effective, and their findings can be understood by only a few analysts. We are surely entitled to ask a few simple questions:

- Rather than putting our trust in complicated and expensive computer models of the future, wouldn't it be interesting to explore what we can learn from ancient, tried-and-tested methods? And to learn how we can apply these to our lives today?
- Rather than prediction being used to sell us things and change our needs and wants, wouldn't it be better if we used it to discover more about ourselves and our place in the world?
- As well as being passively included in other people's statistical surveys, designed to predict how I might behave, could I not use prediction to help me shape and change my own future?
- Would it not be interesting to explore inexpensive methods of prediction, relying on principles which can be grasped by all?

historical Attitudes To Prediction And Oracles

Many people in the West may not now be prepared to consider the possibility of prediction, but its practice was widespread in those cradles of Western civilisation, the ancient Greek and Roman worlds. (Unlike today, in the ancient world it *was* believed that a person's life was determined by fate, or destiny, and that this fate could be revealed. Beliefs such as this died out with the coming of Christianity.)

The ancient Greeks consulted oracles, which they believed to reveal the will of the deities, for all sorts of political and personal purposes. The most famous was the Delphic oracle, where Apollo, the god of foresight, spoke through his priestess. The priestess sat over a cleft in the ground which emitted various vapours. She sat on a tripod and entered a trance-like state, uttering enigmatic words which were then interpreted by a priest. The future was also supposedly revealed by oracular signs, such as the fall of lots or dice, or the appearance of burnt offerings. Dreams were also treated as oracles.

Like the ancient Greeks, the Romans incorporated prediction into their religion and it became highly organised and institutionalised. Indeed, our word *auger*, which as a noun is another name for a soothsayer and as a verb means 'to foresee, predict or portend', comes from the name of a Roman religious official who foretold future events by a variety of methods, including reading the auspices – that is observing the behaviour of birds.

The Ordinariness Of Prophetic Experience

Now that we have set the context for a discussion of prediction, but before we move on to look at the major techniques, it is worth noting the ordinariness of psychic experience generally, and of prophetic experience in particular, and then considering how your psychic ability might affect your success with the methods.

5

See how you score on the following mini-quiz. Answer each question 'Yes' or 'No' by ticking the relevant box.

Yes No

1 Do you ever have unexplained and inexplicable knowledge about the *present*, perhaps through dreams or waking visions?

2 Do you ever have unexplained and inexplicable knowledge about the *past*, (e.g. through a sense of *déjà vu* – the sense that you know a place, or a person, or a thing, even though you have never knowingly encountered them before?

3 Do you ever pick up an object, and simply by holding it learn something about its past, its function, its future?

4 Have you ever felt in advance that you knew something which did happen was going to happen, when there was no rational way that you could have had any foreknowledge of this event?

5 Have you ever felt an inexplicable, vague sense of unease around a person or event, a sense which turned out to be justified?

6 Do you see waking visions of distant places or things, which later turn out to be accurate, even though you had no explicable foreknowledge of them?

7 Do your dreams ever seem to contain messages about the future?

Questions 1, 2 and 3 concern psychic experience generally; questions 4, 5, 6 and 7 concern prophetic experience specifically. It is worth pointing out that questions 1 and 2 concern divinatory knowledge of the past and the present. 'Divination' simply means to discover something by intuition or inspiration, it need not be restricted to knowledge of the future, as is often supposed. All the methods in this book are methods of divination, although we shall be concentrating mainly on prediction – divination of the future.

All of the experiences mentioned in the questions are common. If you answered 'Yes' to any of the questions, especially any of questions 4, 5, 6 and 7, you will probably find yourself receptive to the methods explained in this book. Similarly, if you regularly win at games of chance, can often complete people's sentences before they

do, experience out-of-body states or sometimes smell or hear things when no one else does, then you may have hidden psychic powers and enhanced talents for prediction.

Even if you have no psychic abilities you can still learn to use the methods discussed in this book, at least at beginner's level. However, you may find that the methods seem to you rather mechanical and lifeless, or that they give incomprehensible or contradictory responses to your questions. You may have no inclination for further study.

Why Do Oracles Work?

The question of why methods of prediction work is a thorny one. Different methods work for different reasons and different practitioners have different theories. Brief indications of why I suppose each method might work are given under the subject entries. In general, techniques can be divided into two groups: those that depend on an apparently random throw or spread, such as the I Ching, runes and tarot; and those which are more systematic, such as dream interpretation and numerology.

Let's start by considering methods which rely on an apparently random throw. Here it is relevant to mention a concept first introduced by the psychologist, C. G. Jung. This is the concept of synchronicity which, in effect, introduces the thought that nothing is really random, there are subtle and undetectable non-causal vibrations, connections, call them what you will, linking every event in the universe. So when I consult the I Ching, or the runes, my apparently random throw is, in fact, synchronous with (not caused by) energy balances between yin and yang, my current state of consciousness, or whatever. This means the predictive method provides a powerful snapshot of the universe as it is now and an accurate jumping-off point for thinking about the future.

For more systematic methods, it is often important to remember the power of symbols, magic windows into our subconsciousness which can act as mediators between us and the same mysterious forces of synchronicity, or between us and other people, or between the inner me and the outer me. Often when thinking about the future we need to be able to understand the language of symbols.

7

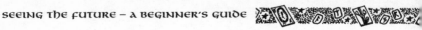

How this book is organised

This book is organised in two parts. In Part One, you will find
practically focused introductions to some of the most well-known
systems of prediction. Use these as pointers on the road to further
study – each section concludes with suggestions for further reading.
The listing of chapters is alphabetical – astrology (Western) through
to tarot. Part Two provides a quick reference dictionary, enabling
you to find definitions of relevant terms, brief details of lesser-known
theories and systems, and some historical and cultural information.

PRACTICE

You will find a practice box at the end of each discussion of a
major divinatory technique. This first box concerns Western
society's use of prediction.

Think up as many business and political situations as you can in
which we, in our modern-day society, try to predict the future.
What methods do we use to predict the future in each case?
How reliable do you think each method is? Is it an expensive
method? Are the principles behind it understood by only a few
people, or available to all? Do you think more accurate methods
of prediction might be available? Why are many people willing to
accept modern methods of prediction in business and politics,
but not ancient methods in their personal lives?

FURTHER READING

You will find suggestions for further reading at the end of each
chapter. Most of the books are to be found in the Beginner's Guide
series (For ordering details see p. ii). Once you have read this
introduction, you might like to read *Your Psychic Powers – a
beginner's guide,* by Craig Hamilton-Parker.

The Major Divination Techniques

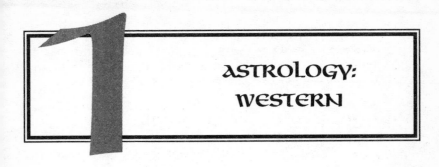

ASTROLOGY: WESTERN

What is astrology?

Astrology can be thought of as the art, not the science, of interpreting a celestial dance – the dance of the sun and moon, the stars and planets. These represent the hidden forces which drive personality, and the patterns they draw in the sky are metaphors for our lives, from birth to death. The whole celestial–human interaction is, perhaps, governed by the mysterious forces of synchronicity, mentioned in the Introduction.

Astrology can help you clarify your thinking about the future and can anticipate potential joys and pitfalls in your life – in your career,

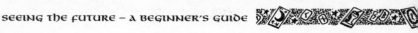

in your relationships, in your financial independence, etc. It can help you to overcome setbacks and work with what you have for maximum fulfilment – sexual, emotional, creative, financial and psychic. It can do so by *helping you to understand yourself a little better.*

Why does astrology work?

Beyond invoking the forces of synchronicity we may never be able to explain why astrology works, but we can begin to edge towards an explanation by thinking about the zodiac. The zodiac is a band of the heavens. Think of it as a necklace with the twelve constellations strung along it like beads: Aries, Taurus, Gemini, Cancer, Leo, Virgo, Libra, Scorpio, Sagittarius, Capricorn, Aquarius and Pisces.

Your sun sign, also sometimes called your star sign, tells you where the sun was positioned in the heavens at the time of your birth. If you are Aries, the sun was in the constellation of Aries; if you are Taurus, it was in Taurus, and so on for the other signs.

Each constellation is governed by one of the planets, the moon or the sun. In ancient times, these celestial bodies were thought to be divine, or at least to possess divine attributes – particular qualities and potentialities. These ancient beliefs gave rise to the idea that different (divinely inspired?) skills are associated with people born under the different constellations. In addition, the constellations are associated with both an element – earth, air, fire or water, and a quality – cardinal, fixed or mutable. These various heavenly associations affect human life via the sun signs.

- Earth signs are sensual.
- Cardinal signs are geared to action.
- Air signs are rational.
- Fixed signs are centred and rooted.
- Fire signs are intuitive.
- Water signs are emotional.
- Mutable signs are adaptable.

The sun is a symbol of the light of consciousness, and it represents the integrating principle of your personality. Knowing a few basic facts about your sun sign gives you a good starting point for astro-psychology and, hence, for using astrology to think about your future. You need to know:

- whether your sun sign is governed by earth, air, fire or water;
- whether your sun sign is fixed, mutable or cardinal;
- which of the celestial bodies governs your sun sign;
- the qualities and potentialities associated with this celestial body.

The following table summarises all this information.

Constellation	Element	Quality	Celestial body	Qualities and potentialities
Aries	Fire	Cardinal	Mars, named for the Roman god of war	Mars is assertive and energetic, highly sexual and passionate. His energy gives us the courage to strike out in new directions and explore new options.
Taurus	Fixed	Earth	Venus, named for the Roman goddess of love	Venus is loving and nurturing, concerned with caring and loyal sexual relationships. On the other hand she is the mistress of tormenting sexual desire.
Gemini	Mutable	Air	Mercury, named for the Roman God of eloquence	Mercury is an eloquent and skilled persuader, with highly honed communication skills and a sharp intellect.
Cancer	Cardinal	Water	The moon	The moon recognises the limitations of reason and the power of intuition and instinct. She is concerned with moods, memory, emotional response, empathy and sympathy.
Leo	Fixed	Fire	The sun	The sun represents the sustaining power of creative energy, the urge to integrate diverse elements into an organic whole, and our moral striving for perfection.
Virgo	Mutable	Earth	Mercury	*See Gemini*

13

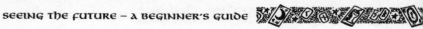

Libra	Cardinal	Air	Venus	*See Taurus*
Scorpio	Fixed	Water	Pluto, named for Greek god of the underworld	Pluto represents transformation and evolution, renewal and elimination. Pluto has an awareness of that which is hidden and can be both jealous and obsessive.
Sagittarius	Mutable	Fire	Jupiter, named for the Roman king of the gods	Jupiter is confident and optimistic, cheerful, freewheeling and unflappable. He is symbolic of expansion and growth.
Capricorn	Cardinal	Earth	Saturn, named for an ancient god of agriculture	Saturn symbolises limitation and discipline, he is down to earth, practical and good with his hands. Saturn is concerned with duty, commitment and responsibility, along with emotional security and insecurity.
Aquarius	Fixed	Air	Uranus, named for a mythical Greek character, son of the earth and father of time	Uranus is rebellious and independent, a progressive thinker, broad minded and tolerant. He is the master of unexpected revelation.
Pisces	Mutable	Water	Neptune, named for the Roman god of the sea	Neptune is idealistic and intuitive, imaginative, dreamy and romantic. He is concerned with compassion, sensitivity and sacrifice.

YOUR BIRTHCHART

In an introductory book such as this, we have space to discuss only your sun sign. *However, the positions of all the planets, and of the*

moon, at the time of your birth also influence your psyche. Your birthchart summarises information about the positions of the planets, the sun and the moon, relative to the zodiac at the time and place of your birth. By revealing the influences of all the celestial bodies, and the relationships between them at the time of your birth when you took on separate existence, your birthchart builds into a complex energy map of your psyche.

ḣow can you use astrology for prediction?

When thinking about the future, you can begin to use astrology simply by contemplating the powers and influences of and on your sun sign. This might provide you with useful leads, for example if your sunsign is governed by Mars, you might need to solve problems in the future by working with aggression – either increasing it, perhaps by becoming more assertive, or decreasing it, perhaps by trying to control your violent temper. If Pluto is your ruling planet, in the future you may need to try to moderate the intensity of your reactions, say in a romantic entanglement, and try to recognise that others do not see things in such desperate lights as you. If Venus is your ruling planet, you may need to focus on how and why you can harness the power of your sexuality in the future.

It is not possible for an absolute beginner to go much further than this; if you require a greater level of predictive detail, you should have your birthchart drawn up by an experienced and reputable astrologer.

Troubleshooting

Even a reliable and experienced astrologer can produce a misleading birthchart, for at least two reasons:

- You may have provided slightly inaccurate information about the place and/or time of your birth, which will have led to inaccuracies in calculating the positions of the celestial bodies at the time of your birth. Thus, there will be inaccuracies in interpreting their powers and influences, and the relationships between them.

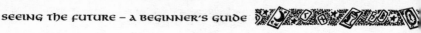

- You may have misunderstood what your astrologer told you. If you are in any doubt about any point during a consultation, stop your astrologer and ask her or him to explain. Your birthchart is supposed to enlighten you, not confuse you.

The general horoscopes offered in newspapers and magazines are often inaccurate, because they cater to all Geminis, or all Scorpios, and do not take into account the place and exact time of birth of each Gemini or Scorpio who might be reading the column. Nevertheless, they can contain useful psychological insights and hints about the day, or week, or month ahead.

Limitations

Whenever, and however, you choose to use astrology, it is important to remember that it is a system of understanding which does not, and could not, rob you either of your own free will or of responsibility for your actions. Events are not literally written in the stars, rather psychic energies are hinted at, or suggested. Every one of your freely chosen actions could set off a chain of events with profound consequences for you and your loved ones.

SUCCESS STORY

Liz had no knowledge of astrology, beyond the fact that her sun sign was Sagittarius. A friend persuaded her to have her birthchart drawn-up. This revealed that Sagittarius governed most aspects of Liz's life – love, money, health and career. It is most unusual for so many aspects of life to be governed by one constellation. Liz was aware of some of the implications of this, through odd facts she had picked up about her sun sign – she recognised that she was always chasing arrows, that her honesty sometimes led her into tactlessness and that she was a good leader. But she now found herself dissecting her character in a self-conscious way and thinking about how she could harness the energy of Sagittarius to produce fulfilment and satisfaction. At work, she tried to moderate her obvious lack of respect for some of her colleagues. In all spheres of her life she attempted to prioritise between conflicting demands and projects. She now feels that she sets herself achievable goals, rather than chasing unachievable dreams, and this has led to

career and personal benefits. She has recognised and embraced the Sagittarius inclination for sports, something she previously suppressed, to the great improvement of her health.

pRACTICE

This exercise is designed to increase your awareness of the influence of your governing celestial body, remembering that the ancients thought of these as divine. Set yourself the challenge of finding out all you can about the deity associated with your sun sign. Browse in the mythology section of the local library. Your local museum may have a collection of Greek or Roman artefacts, which might depict the deity concerned. Or has your deity been adopted by a modern organisation? For example, Mercury, god of communication, is the name and emblem of one of Britain's largest telecommunications organisations. What patterns in your own life which seem to be relevant to your new discoveries? Do they shock you, or make you uneasy? There are no right or wrong answers here; the purpose of the exercise is simply to open your eyes to the net of possibilities spread by your deity.

fURThER READING

The following books in this series give more detailed information on topics covered in this chapter: *Astrology* by Graham Boston; *Astrology and Health* by Dylan Warren-Davis; *Love Signs* by Kristyna Arcarti; *Money Signs* by Chisteen Skinner; *Star Signs* by Kristyna Arcarti; *The Moon and You* by Teresa Moorey.

Also of interest are:

Teach Yourself Astrology by Jeff Mayo and Christine Ramsdale, published by Hodder & Stoughton, 1997
Reach Your Potential by Teresa Moorey – a series of twelve books, one for each star sign, which use astropsychology to show you how to make the best of yourself and your talents. Published by Hodder & Stoughton, 1998.

CHINESE WISDOM: I CHING AND ASTROLOGY

WHAT ARE I CHING AND CHINESE ASTROLOGY?

I Ching, the Chinese oracle of changes, and Chinese lunar astrology are distinct systems, but both link into, are formed by and help to form an enormously complex web of thinking, encompassing religion, cosmology, science, philosophy, medicine and art. This web is spun around a basic duality of yin – masculine, light, warm, strong – and yang – female, yielding, dark, cool. Yin and yang are the two primeval forces of nature.

I Ching

Stripped down to its most basic form, the I Ching is composed of sixty-four six-line hexagrams, made up of broken and unbroken lines (p. 23). Yin is represented by broken lines, yang by unbroken lines. Each hexagram represents different balances between yin and yang in dynamic situations of flux and change, and each has been given an interpretation in the book of changes. These interpretations are couched in allegorical, poetical language – the I Ching speaks in metaphors. You use the interpretations to analyse states of change in your own life, to help you understand them and respond by making suitable and relevant decisions.

Chinese astrology

Unlike Western astrology, Chinese astrology does not study the movement of the heavenly bodies across the sky, but rather concentrates on the passage of whole years through time. The New Year celebrated by Chinese communities throughout the world is a new *lunar* year. Each lunar year is governed by an animal, which shows specific characteristics. Each animal is either yin or yang, and its characteristics can be modified by one of five elements – wood, water, earth, fire or metal. According to this system, each one of us shows characteristics of one of the animals, modified by one of the elements, depending on the year and month of our birth.

Why do these systems work?

I Ching

The I Ching works because it allows you to access your own intuitive powers, and bring your own creativity to decision making – think of it as a tool to allow you to communicate with yourself. You already have the answers to the questions you are asking hidden in your subconscious, and the oracle helps you to gain focus and clarity, thus enabling you to bring those answers to consciousness and recognise their power.

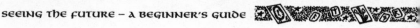
LOWER TRIGRAMS ╲ UPPER TRIGRAMS	☰	☱	☳	☲	☷	☶	☵	☴
☰	1	43	34	14	11	26	5	9
☱	10	58	54	38	19	41	60	61
☳	25	17	51	21	24	27	3	42
☲	13	49	55	30	36	22	63	37
☷	12	45	16	35	2	23	8	20
☶	33	31	62	56	15	52	39	53
☵	6	47	40	64	7	4	29	59
☴	44	28	32	50	46	18	48	57

Chinese astrology

The Chinese system describes at least sixty different personality types (twelve animals, modified by five elements: 12 × 5 = 60). This is the minimum. As well as the dominant animal, each of us also has a companion animal and a hidden animal. In the hands of skilled practitioners, Chinese astrology works because of its complexity, flexibility and ability to acknowledge variations, enabling the practitioner to draw up a highly specific, individual picture of his or her client's life energy.

how can you use these systems for prediction?

I Ching

I Ching is the oldest book-oracle in the world, dating back at least 3000 years, probably 4000 years. The original interpretations of the hexagrams – diagrams of yin and yang in dynamic states of change – were given by sages and holy men. The hexagrams were probably initially derived by throwing yarrow sticks and it is still possible to consult the oracle this way. But it is far simpler to use coins or dice – or even to click on a computer mouse.

You start by formulating your question as clearly as you can. Formulating your question clearly is the first step towards the sort of mental clarity and objectivity which the I Ching promotes as a means to stimulating your intuition. It is generally better to couch your questions in positive terms, than negative (e.g. ask what to do, rather than what not to do).

Once you have formulated your question, you need a means of capturing in diagrammatic form the balance of yin and yang at this instant – you need a kind of snapshot of the flux of your own subconscious in the world, now. As mentioned earlier, there are various methods of achieving this – including the modern method of clicking a mouse and letting your computer generate the hexagram. But perhaps the easiest method is to use a die.

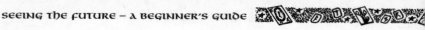

Throw a die six times, each time making a note of the number you throw. Assign yin to even numbers and yang to odd numbers. Draw the yin (broken) or yang (unbroken) line for the first number you threw at the *bottom* of the hexagram and add each of the other five lines *above* it in order – as shown below. The bottom three lines are called the bottom trigram, the top three the upper trigram.

Use any copy of the I Ching (or see page 20) to determine which hexagram you have created. Most copies of the I Ching have a key showing combinations of the upper and lower trigrams, and look up the relevant interpretation. Any translation of the I Ching will serve your purposes. Use the interpretation given in your copy of the I Ching as a key to unlock your own powers of intuition and to release a flood of creative thinking on the situation in which you find yourself.

Sample hexagram

Number of throw	Number thrown	Hexagram	Hexagram number and meaning
6	4	– – –	
5	2	– – –	11 – good
4	6	– – –	fortune
3	5	——	lies ahead.
2	3	——	
1	3	——	

Chinese astrology

The complexities of Chinese astrology mean it is not possible for beginners to draw up horoscopes. But, as a first step towards exploring this intricate intellectual system, you can begin to reflect on the meaning of your governing animal in your life, and to see

how its characteristics manifest, or fail to manifest, in you. Look up the animal governing the year of your birth in the table opposite then use the following classification as a spur to set you thinking – only minimal information is given here. **NB**: Those born in January or February may feel that they are not, in fact, a hare (or whatever), even though this is the animal indicated for their year of birth. This inaccuracy creeps in because the Chinese lunar year does not correspond directly to the Western calendar year. If you find yourself in this situation, the animal governing the preceding or following lunar year may have messages for you.

- Rat – Yang. Charming, charismatic, intelligent, sociable and friendly. Likes risk.
- Ox – Yin. Stable, sensible, solid, strong and tenacious. Quite materialistic.
- Tiger – Yang. Forceful, compulsive, brave, ferocious. Does not suffer fools gladly.
- Hare – Yin. Secretive, mysterious, creative, artistic. Associated with both fertility and immortality.
- Dragon – Yang. Leaders and persuaders. Honesty borders on tactlessness. Does not like taking orders.
- Snake – Yin. Wise, discreet and cultured. Masters of understatement, shrewd financiers.
- Horse -Yang. Sporty, good-looking, extrovert and smart. Loves to be the centre of attention, but hates to be ignored.
- Goat – Yin. Sensitive, altruistic, anxious. Incapable of quitting a task. A protector.
- Monkey – Yang. Active, agile and busy. Intelligent, obstinate and quick tempered.
- Rooster – Yin. Those born near dawn are noisy and think they are always right. Those born later are more withdrawn.
- Dog – Yang. Loyal and unselfish, needs love and affection. Disconsolate if they feel unwanted.
- Pig – Yin. Tolerant, sincere, easy going and placid. Fond of food and drink, can be self-indulgent.

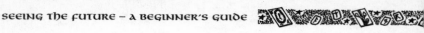

The animal years

Animal									
Rat	1900	1912	1924	1936	1948	1960	1972	1984	1996
Ox	1901	1913	1925	1937	1949	1961	1973	1985	1997
Tiger	1902	1914	1926	1938	1950	1962	1974	1986	1998
Rabbit	1903	1915	1927	1939	1951	1963	1975	1987	1999
Dragon	1904	1916	1928	1940	1952	1964	1976	1988	2000
Snake	1905	1917	1929	1941	1953	1965	1977	1989	2001
Horse	1906	1918	1930	1942	1954	1966	1978	1990	2002
Goat	1907	1919	1931	1943	1955	1967	1979	1991	2003
Monkey	1908	1920	1932	1944	1956	1968	1980	1992	2004
Rooster	1909	1921	1933	1945	1957	1969	1981	1993	2005
Dog	1910	1922	1934	1946	1958	1970	1982	1994	2006
Pig	1911	1923	1935	1947	1959	1971	1983	1995	2007

Troubleshooting

I Ching

If the I Ching appears to be giving contradictory, irrelevant, or simply incomprehensible advice, ask yourself the following three questions.

1 Did I formulate my question as clearly as possible? If your question is clear, the advice is also likely to be clear. If your question is muddled, the advice is also likely to be muddled. In part, this is because, unless the question is clear, it is easy and often tempting to analyse the interpretation of the hexagram in terms slightly different from the terms in which you posed the question – this is especially true if you have a strong desire for one possible interpretation to dominate another.
2 What was my state of mind when I posed my question? If you are in deep conflict when you posed your question, then the snapshot of yin and yang as it relates to your subconscious at this instant – the hexagram – will reflect this conflict. Suppose you asked a question relating to office politics, but you were also worried about a row you recently had with your partner, however clearly you posed your question about the office, the balance of yin and yang in your mind, and hence in the hexagram, would reflect your worry about your partner – hence the oracle's advice would be confused.
3 Do I have any motive for wanting one interpretation rather than another? We already touched on this earlier. If you desperately want the I Ching to analyse your situation in a given way, that will influence your reflections on the interpretation and make it harder for you to see its underlying meaning.

Chinese astrology

If you had your horoscope drawn up by a Chinese astrologer and it seemed inaccurate, the same considerations apply as in Western astrology – see p. 16.

LIMITATIONS

I Ching

Remember that the I Ching – the book of *changes* (not of *outcomes*) cannot predict that any event will happen with certainty. Rather it is a tool for decision making which unlocks your own powers of intuition and insight, enabling you to analyse the possible qualities of future events, and to judge likelihoods.

Chinese astrology

Chinese astrology, like Western astrology, cannot reveal the future, but merely offers an insight into various possibilities and options. Like Western astrology it is at least as concerned with psychoanalysis as with prediction – at an introductory level it is best regarded as a tool for self-understanding.

SUCCESS STORY

You can use I Ching to help with any form of decision making – at home, at work, in your most intimate relationships, etc. Susan uses the I Ching to help her manage her relationship with her difficult teenage daughter, Diane. Diane frequently tests her mother by remaining out late, picking fights and answering back. Susan finds that she is able to remain composed through these situations by using the I Ching to help her reflect on her state of mind, her long- and short-term relationships with her daughter and the wider implications of Diane's behaviour. She uses it as a means of centring herself when engaged in delicate parent–child negotiations. You can use it as a method of centring yourself whenever you are engaged in challenging negotiations, of any type.

PRACTICE 1

I CHING

The practice exercise is on formulating questions. Choose an issue which is troubling you – perhaps your career is stalled, or relations with your partner have gone a bit stale. Whatever you choose, you need to be prepared to discuss this issue with a close friend, or loved one. Formulate two or three questions concerning your chosen issue. Then sit down with a friend and ask whether they understand your questions. Are they absolutely clear? Or are your questions ambiguous? If so, why? Allow your friend to help you to clarify your questions. This is excellent practice for formulating questions for the I Ching. If you cannot pose your questions in such a way that someone else can understand them, you probably cannot pose them in such a way to facilitate a genuine conversation with yourself, mediated by the I Ching.

PRACTICE 2

CHINESE ASTROLOGY

Start to keep a scrap book and fill it with pictures of the animal governing your year of birth. Jot down any thoughts the images bring to mind. This will encourage you to start thinking about your animal in all its peculiarity and complexity. As you do so, your understanding of its life energy and life patterns will deepen and you may find this understanding can be brought to bear on challenges in your own life.

FURTHER READING

The following books in this series give more detailed information on topics covered in this chapter.

Chinese Horoscopes by Kristyna Arcarti
Feng Shui and *Feng Shui – a complete guide,* both by Richard Craze
I Ching by Kristyna Arcarti

Also:

Teach Yourself Chinese Astrology by Richard Craze with Billy Lee
Teach Yourself Traditional Chinese Medicine by Richard Craze
Teach Yourself Feng Shui by Richard Craze

all published by Hodder & Stoughton, 1998.

3 CRYSTAL MAGIC

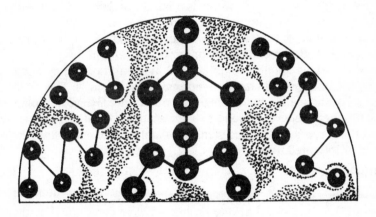

What is crystal magic?

Ordinary stones, precious and semi-precious gems and crystals have been used in divination since ancient times. The most well-known forms are *scrying* – the practice of gazing into a clear quartz crystal ball to promote visions – and *lithomancy* – the practice of casting stones and using the patterns they form as a basis for prediction.

Scrying, which was probably introduced to Europe by the Romans, almost certainly developed from ancient practices of gazing into reflective surfaces, such as water or black ink. Since the cost of true, polished-quartz crystal balls is prohibitive today and, since cheaper glass balls do not give the same results, you can use a bowl of water for the exercise given later in this chapter.

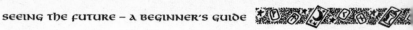

Lithomancy has ancient and obscure origins. Various forms of lot casting are known from ancient times, such as casting grain, shells or bones. Casting stones was simply an alternative method.

Why do scrying and Lithomancy work?

Scrying

The way in which scrying works is a matter of debate, but it seems probable that through gazing into a reflective surface the scryer induces a state of trance in him or her self. Trance can be regarded as a state of disassociation of consciousness and in this state, psychic powers are able to function at maximum potential, freed from the background chatter of normal consciousness. This enables the scryer to see visions in his or her mind's eye. However, some practitioners believe the reflective surface itself creates the images and the scryer's heightened state of psychic awareness merely helps in their interpretation.

Lithomancy

In the ancient world, it was believed that any form of casting the lots worked because the patterns created were determined by divine powers – this method was used to determine the will of the deities. (who were themselves, to a large extent, subject to fate, or destiny). Casting lots was frequently used to discover whom the deities desired to fulfil a particular role – a practice reflected in our phrase 'my lot in life'. A modern spin on the ancient explanation of how the lots worked is to suggest that the apparently random patterns created are, in fact, synchronous with powerful yet undetectable forces surging round us – the forces of synchronicity (see the Introduction). Perhaps the lottery – a modern method of casting the lots – selects winners of cash in this way.

how do you use scrying and Lithomancy?

Scrying

Traditionally, scrying with a crystal ball is performed at night, either at the time of the full moon or during its waxing. This is not practical for beginners, who want to practise their technique and, in any case, a bowl of water will not react to lunar energy in the same way as quartz, so just ensure that you practise scrying at a time when you can guarantee peace and quite – preferably silence.

Mental health check

Do not attempt scrying if you have a history of mental illness, are taking any medication for any type of mental illness, are under severe stress, have recently suffered a bereavement, or are generally miserable. Nor should you attempt scrying if you feel uncomfortable with the idea of self-hypnosis. You should be in a generally happy, confident frame of mind when undertaking scrying.

It is not necessary to formulate a question, but you can do so if you prefer. If you want to pose a question, read the notes under 'I Ching' in Chapter 2 and do the Practice exercise given there.

Make sure the light is dim and that the atmosphere is neither too hot nor too cool. You must sit in a comfortable position, with your back well supported. Breathe evenly and deeply for a few minutes prior to gazing into your bowl of water. Try to shut out the chatter of your mind.

When you are ready, gaze into your bowl of water. The bowl itself should be plain, preferably of a dark colour, with no distracting patterns. You may see nothing – indeed, for your first few attempts you will almost certainly see nothing. The first sign of visions is usually a clouding in the water. Once you have seen this clouding,

you may start to see visions. Make a careful note of anything you see, be as detailed as possible. Do not write 'I saw a dove', but 'I saw a white dove, with silver tips to its feathers, flying across the sky from east to west, carrying a leaf in its beak'.

You must try to interpret whatever you see in the light of the issue, or the question, concerning you. For example, if you were worried about a friend whom you had not seen for many years, the message of the dove might be that you would soon receive news, or possibly that you might make a journey to see him or her soon – certainly, it conveys hope. Only *you* can interpret *your* visions, and interpretation depends on the skilful analysis of symbols – for more on this see 'Dream interpretation', Chapter 5.

Write down your interpretation alongside your description of the relevant vision. Use this careful record to check the accuracy of any predictions you make. But remember to guard against temptation to interpret visions in a way which suits your current purposes and plans. You are likely to be looking for connections between your past visions and events that actually occur – beware of this tendency to try to prove your scrying is effective.

Lithomancy

There are many methods of lithomancy. This is one of the simplest, giving straightforward yes/no answers to the questions you choose to pose.

Gather thirty stones of roughly equal size, shape and texture from your garden or other patch of ground. Put a dot of paint on fifteen of them. Once your stones are prepared, place them all in a cloth bag, then formulate your question, which must be capable of being answered with yes or no. Shake the cloth bag. Close your eyes, reach in and grab a handful of stones. If you have pulled out more stones with paint dots on them than without, the answer to your question is *yes*. If you have pulled out more stones without dots on them than with dots, the answer is *no*. If you have pulled out an equal number of stones with and without dots, reformulate your question slightly differently, remembering that any question must be capable of a yes/no answer. If you cannot reformulate your question,

or if you once again pull out equal numbers of stones with and without dots, your question cannot yet be answered, at least in yes/no terms.

Troubleshooting

Scrying

If, after a few weeks of practising scrying on a regular basis, you have seen no visions, then try freeing-up your subconscious mind using the following exercise. Lie down, in a quite, warm and dark room, then breath deeply, close your eyes and count backwards from 100 – the worst that can happen is that you fall asleep. After practising this technique, do you find that you see visions when scrying? If not, perhaps scrying is not for you. If you see visions, but they seem to have no relevance to your life, remember it is always difficult to interpret allegorical, metaphorical or symbolic messages.

Lithomancy

Because it gives simple yes/no answers, it is easy to spot when lithomancy gets it wrong. If this happens regularly, remember that most issues in life are too complicated to reduce to yes/no, and use casting the stones to supplement to your decision making – one piece of advice, one consideration, amongst many.

Limitations

Neither scrying nor lithomancy can predict events with certainty. Like all other methods, they can only indicate possibilities and likelihood. Your fate, such as it is, is in your hands. You, and only you, remain responsible for the choices and decisions you take. It can appear a limitation of lithomancy, that it can give answers to only yes/no questions, but think of this as a powerful incentive for you to think through a given issue and articulate your questions at their most basic level – a good exercise in mental clarity which will start to unleash the creative potential of your own mind to produce

some possible answers. If you have difficulty formulating your concerns in yes/no format, try the exercise in the Practice box under 'Dowsing', Chapter 4.

SUCCESS STORY

Once a year Barbara consults a psychic who uses scrying in his consultations – he has a genuine quartz crystal ball, passed down through generations of his gypsy family. Barbara has always found his predictions accurate, over a range of subjects as diverse as when she and her husband would move house – 10 months after the date of the consultation – and where the new house would be, to the date and nature of a promotion for her daughter's husband and upheavals in her husband's career – he went freelance. The psychic also correctly predicted improvements in Barbara's health and prompted her to start hormone replacement therapy to ease her transition through the menopause, a move she found highly beneficial.

FURTHER READING

The following books in this series give more detailed information on topics covered in this chapter.

Gems and Crystals by Kristyna Arcarti
Witchcraft by Teresa Moorey

PRACTICE

SCRYING

Try to become aware of the properties of reflective surfaces around you. Mirrors and shop windows are likely to reflect your own image. How does that image look to you? Like you? Or not? Try to go to a fairground hall of mirrors. What do the mirrors there do to your image? When you have the opportunity, gaze into pools, polished metal, or any other highly polished surface. What images are brought to mind. Do they have any significance for you? Or not? Informally becoming aware of reflective surfaces and the images they reflect, project, conjure up, hide, distort, shrink or magnify will help you to develop your formal scrying skills.

LITHOMANCY

Try to develop sensitivity to the energy of stones. Hold a common garden stone in your hand. How old do you think it is? How was it formed? Where did it come from? If you can, get hold of a piece of amethyst, rose quartz, garnet, or any semi-precious stone which appeals to you. How does it feel in your hand, warm or cool? How does it reflect light? Does it feel smooth or rough? Stones are wonderful and amazing things. If you appreciate them, your sympathetic energy can perhaps influence the efficacy of lithomancy.

4 · DOWSING

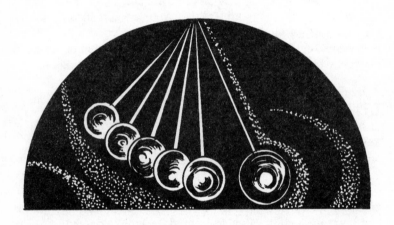

What is Dowsing?

Dowsing is best known as a means of detecting that which is hidden – hidden water, oil or minerals, hidden objects thought lost forever, hidden archaeological sites, hidden illness or disturbance in the aura, etc. Dowsing rods made of metal or wood – typically forked twigs – are particularly associated with this type of dowsing, the rods dip suddenly when held over the right spot. But dowsing can also be used as an aid to decision making, to help us uncover options hidden deep within our conscious or subconscious minds. Pendulums are usually used for this sort of dowsing and we shall concentrate on dowsing with pendulums in this chapter.

Why does dowsing work?

The basic premise of dowsing is that everything consists of energy. The dowsing rods, or the pendulum, somehow act as conduits between the psychic energy of the person seeking that which is lost and the energy emitted by that which is sought – be it a physical thing, an answer to a difficult question, or the source of ill health. The seeker can use his or her imagination to direct psychic energy by visualising that which is to be found, if it is a thing, or formulating a clear question, if it is an answer.

How can you use dowsing for prediction?

You can make a pendulum using any small object that can be tied to string. Stones and crystals, buttons, rings or coins can all be used. Some Native Americans use arrow heads. Make sure that you use string made of natural fibre, not nylon. Your pendulum should be between 15 and 20 centimetres (6 and 8 inches) long.

Sit down at a table, hold the pendulum between your thumb and forefinger, in your right hand if you are right-handed, in your left hand if you are left-handed. Rest your elbow on the table top, to give stability. Ask a simple yes/no question to which you already know the answer (Am I a man?) and wait. The pendulum should soon begin to swing. The direction of the swing will determine your yes/no direction. If you are a man, and the pendulum swings clockwise, that is your yes direction. If you are a woman and it swings clockwise, that is your no direction. If the pendulum swings from side to side, or remains still, repeat the exercise until you have determined your yes/no directions. To be sure of your yes/no direction, you should repeat the exercise a few times, with more questions to which you know the answer – is a duck a fish? Is the earth square?

You can now go on to ask questions to which you desire an answer. If the pendulum does not move, or swings backwards and forwards,

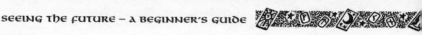

with no clear clockwise/anti-clockwise direction, try to phrase the question in a different way – it must still have a yes/no format. If after you have re-phrased the question a few times the pendulum still provides no clear answer, no clear answer can yet be produced.

TROUBLESHOOTING

If your pendulum never seems to move, or swings backwards and forwards, or does not seem to have a consistent yes/no direction, try making a new pendulum. Use a small object that has significance for you – a ring, a lucky talisman, a treasured stone, or whatever. Make sure you use string made of natural fibre, and use a slightly longer length.

LIMITATIONS

Like lithomancy (see Chapter 3), dowsing can give answers only to yes/no questions; this can appear a limitation, but can also be a powerful incentive for you to think through a given issue and articulate your questions at their most basic level – a good exercise in mental clarity which will start to unleash the creative potential of your own mind to produce some possible answers. Dowsing cannot predict events with certainty, but it can be used to aid decision making. You can use the answers which come from within your own mind, mediated by the pendulum, in conjunction with other deliberations when deciding how to proceed in your life.

SUCCESS STORY

Ron, a keen gardener, had successfully used dowsing rods to help him to find an underground stream running beneath his garden, and also to help him to plan an irrigation system. Encouraged by his experience with rods, Ron decided to try the pendulum method to help him to make garden-related decisions. He asked such questions as whether he should rip out his rose bed and replant it as a Mediterranean border (yes – he now has a wonderful border filled with herbs and flowers in

*the colours of the South, deep blues, yellows and reds) and whether a
certain type of climbing rose would flourish if he planted it by the gate
(no – he planted it by the wall instead). He now regards his pendulum
as an essential aid to garden design and planning.*

PRACTICE

This exercise concentrates on articulating yes/no questions. Re-
phrase the following questions in yes/no form. For most of them, you
will need to use at least two yes/no questions to capture the essence
of the more complex question.

- 'If I decide to move, would it be better for me to take a flat
  than a house, and should I be in the centre of town, or not?'

- 'Why do I get so moody around J?'

- 'Does J's behaviour towards me mean (s)he no longer loves
  me, or is just under stress at the moment?'

- 'How can I cut my monthly expenses, so that I can save a
  little money each month?'

- 'What do I need to do to win promotion at work?'

It may seem impossible to get to the core of some issues using
yes/no questions. But if you persevere, you can usually find
questions to ask. If not, perhaps the decision, or the issue, facing
you is best approached by other means.

FURTHER READING

The following books in this series give more detailed information on
topics covered in this chapter.

Dowsing by Naomi Ozaniec
Earth Mysteries by Teresa Moorey

5 DREAM INTERPRETATION

WHAT IS DREAM INTERPRETATION?

To interpret is 'to bring the meaning out of something' – be it a foreign language, a difficult text or a dream. Dream interpretation simply means uncovering the meanings locked within the sometimes strange, sometimes awe-inspiring, sometimes terrifying, but always fascinating images we see in our dreams. The skilled interpreter of dreams can often find divinatory or prophetic messages in dream imagery – dreams were often treated as oracles in ancient times.

Why does dream interpretation work?

We can think about this in the following ways:

- Every human emotion, desire, experience, quality and possibility can be reflected in dreams – this is the realm where parts of our minds normally held in check by reason, and the day-to-day demands of living are dominant, giving us glimpses of a kind of reality at a tangent to the reality we encounter in our waking hours.
- The subconscious mind has the power to dramatise and to analyse problems, and assimilate material in a way we cannot comprehend with our conscious minds. In dreams, this power can be brought to bear on problems connected with our life now, in the past and in the future.
- Skilful interpretation of dreams requires an ability to look beneath, beyond and around the surface meanings of words or images. It requires the ability to see those words or images as symbols, standing in the place of some other reality. The images we see in dreams are (usually) symbols; if we worry away at these symbols, peeling back layers and layers of meaning we can, often, although not always, arrive at what they truly mean for us.

How can you use dream interpretation for prediction?

Prophetic dreams can offer warnings, make suggestions about important events, give straightforward factual predictions, suggest inspired paths of action in any sphere of life – business, personal, artistic, health, etc. But how can we utilise the power of dreams – that is, the power of our own subconscious minds – when taking decisions about the future?

There are three steps to dream interpretation:

- recalling dreams
- recognising significant dreams
- interpreting dreams.

To help with all three steps, you need to start a dream diary. This can be written or recorded on to tape. The important thing is that your means of recording dreams should be easy to use and easily accessible when you wake. A cheap exercise book is sufficient for a written diary – keep it, and a supply of pens, by your bed. Immediately you wake up, jot down, or record, any dream images or themes which remain with you, and any ideas, thoughts or feelings these images and themes inspire.

Significant dreams

Recognising significant dreams can be difficult. A dream following over-indulgence in food or alcohol could be vivid, while containing little of symbolic meaning. The same applies to a dream obviously influenced by a book you have read, or a film or play you have seen. Dreams influenced by your immediate physical surroundings are also unlikely to have psychological significance – for example, if you dream of water tumbling over rocks and, on waking, realise the tap in your room has been dripping all night, or if you dream of the buzzing of a swarm of bees, only to wake up and realise that a piece of electrical equipment is buzzing.

Other types of dream are nearly always significant – recurring dreams, nightmares, sexual dreams, dreams of dead relatives or significant figures in your life. Keeping a dream diary over several months, watching for patterns and eliminating obviously irrelevant dreams, will help build your ability to recognise significant dreams. You are the judge of what is significant for you, so if a dream seems significant to you, it is. But remember that a significant dream need not have *prophetic* significance – it could reveal something about the past, confirm something you suspect about the present, offer an inspirational solution to an intellectual problem, etc.

Interpreting dreams

Once you are skilled in recalling your dreams and in recognising significant ones, how do you interpret them? Start by identifying the main theme or image, and also all sub-themes or images. For example, if you dream of a circus, the most important image may be of the big top being erected, or collapsing; it may be of one of the

acts – clowns, trapeze artists, etc.; it may be of the man selling candy-floss at the entrance. Alternatively, any of these could be a minor theme, as could images of the audience, of the ringmaster, of any musicians. Start with the main theme, try to understand it and then move on to consider lesser themes.

Remember that your dream images are symbols – they are like smoky windows on to a world where different rules apply – time can move in any direction, objects can fly through space with ease or pass through each other. They are visual, not verbal, riddles, metaphors and allegories produced by your subconscious mind. In interpretation, your conscious mind must convert them into verbal statements, capable of being understood literally. In effect, your conscious mind must crack a code devised by your subconscious mind.

There are no right or wrong meanings to symbols – *you* determine their meaning for *you*. The only way to determine meaning is to reflect on the symbol itself – take the image of a ringmaster. This could stand for:

- any person with power in your life
- any person at the hub of any activity
- your desire to be the centre of attention
- your desire to control events
- power itself
- control itself
- none of these.

Once you have recorded your dreams, start jotting down ideas that come into your head when you ponder the images you saw. Patterns, interpretations and the relevance of the dream images to your life should start to emerge – they may not be clear patterns at first, the relevance may seem minimal or the interpretation arbitrary, but as you continue to work with your dreams, your skill and confidence will increase.

TROUBLESHOOTING

If you have trouble recalling dreams on waking, try priming yourself before you go to sleep. Tell yourself that you will recall your dreams,

or even suggest a potential topic to yourself. If you still fail to recall any dreams, try setting your alarm clock to go off in the night – you may find that your sleep has been interrupted at a fruitful moment, enabling you to recall dreams vividly. This method is not practical for long-term use and your partner may object!

If you have problems interpreting your dreams, remember that practice makes perfect. Some symbols may seem particularly obscure – not every symbol is capable of interpretation. If you really cannot understand a symbol, set this image aside and wait for the underlying meaning to present itself in more intelligible form in a later dream.

Limitations

Dreams are messages from your subconscious mind. Even prophetic dreams cannot literally foretell the future. But they can offer you hints and possibilities and awaken you to ideas, concepts and options you would not otherwise have considered.

SUCCESS STORY

Our subconscious mind has the ability to detect physical changes in our bodies long before any outward signs appear. For example, many women have dreams suggesting they might be pregnant before this is confirmed. Or dreams may convey warnings of illness, or of physical weakness which may present a problem in the distant future. Bob, an apparently healthy man in his mid-30s, had recurring dreams of breathing difficulties and restriction round his chest. After several months he took this warning seriously and had a full-scale health check-up. This revealed that his cholesterol level was way above average and that smoking was having a seriously detrimental effect on his lung capacity and efficiency. Bob was frightened enough to make long-resisted changes to his diet and lifestyle. Thus he lowered some controllable risk factors for heart disease.

PRACTICE

This exercise is to help develop your interpretative skills, and works on the assumption that trying to understand abstract art can be a bit like trying to understand dreams.

Take a trip to your local art gallery and wander round the rooms containing abstract art. Choose one piece which particularly appeals to you – it need not be a picture, a sculpture might draw your attention. Look at it for as long as possible. Look from every angle, from different distances. What do you think the artist was trying to express through this piece? Was it a message capable of literal interpretation, or not? Was it about things, people, or events? What about shape and form? What other images does it suggest to you? How does it relate to the pieces around it in the gallery?

If you cannot get to an art gallery, try to obtain a book containing pictures of modern art – your local library should be able to acquire one for you. Use a reproduction in the book instead of an original. But think about how reproduction might have altered your perception of the piece – does it look tiny, when the text tells you it is 3 metres (10 feet) by 4 metres (13 feet)? Or does it look huge, when the text tells you it is only 2.5 centimetres (2 inches) inches across? Do you think the reproduction of colours is accurate? What about texture?

FURTHER READING

The following books in this series give more detailed information on topics covered in this chapter.

Dream Interpretation by Michele Simmons and Chris McLaughlin
Interpreting Signs and Symbols by Kristyna Arcarti

Also:

Teach Yourself Dream Interpretation by Leila Bright, to be published by Hodder & Stoughton in 1999

6 NATURAL PHENOMENA

WHAT IS DIVINATION BY NATURAL PHENOMENA?

Using phenomena encountered in the natural world as tools for prediction is an ancient practice and evidence for it is found all over the world. Almost any natural phenomena can be used. Here we will look briefly at the role of water, lightning, the stars and moon, wind and clouds, the flight of birds, fire and plants and trees.

Why do these methods work?

These methods work in various ways, and all are open to debate. Beyond referring to the connections of synchronicity (see the Introduction), we can perhaps consider that mother earth and father sky (or, as some traditions would have it, father earth and mother sky) have protected, kept and nourished humans since they first appeared on earth. Perhaps, if we are prepared to study some of the gifts mother earth and father sky have granted us, they will tolerate our tapping into their energies and wisdom, enabling us to think about our own lives and futures in constructive and innovative ways.

How can you use natural phenomena for prediction?

Water

We have already looked at divination using water under 'Scrying', in Chapter 3. In addition to scrying, the way in which objects float or sink in water can be used to answer 'yes/no' questions, and this idea underlies many divinatory practices. For example, one method, said to have its origins in Polynesia, is to place a small flower in the bottom of a bowl, formulate your yes/no question, pour clean, cold water over the flower and watch whether it rises, or remains at the bottom. If the flower floats, the answer is yes, if it stays at the bottom, the answer is no. If it rises, then sinks again, no answer is yet possible.

Lightning

Lightning, one of the most powerful forces of nature, has always inspired awe, and has often been used for divinatory purposes. In ancient Rome, for example, the brightness, proximity and type of lightning were all used to predict the success of a newly established household. However, for simple practical reasons it can be a difficult

and unreliable method – you cannot provoke lightning, and it can usually be observed only under difficult storm conditions. If you are inclined to do so, and both accept the risk of, and take precautions against, being struck by lightning, go outside on a night that will probably produce lightning. Stand facing any direction, waiting for the first flash. If it appears to your left, this portends trouble. If it appears to the right, this portends good fortune. If no lightning appears, or it is directly over head, this indicates neutrality between trouble and good fortune.

Stars

Star divination is used throughout the world and is very ancient. Western astrology uses star divination (see Chapter 1). Shooting stars, meteorites and comets have long been considered of great significance, even in our own time – as shown by the excitement caused by the 1997 sightings of comet Hale-Bopp. Shooting stars have been said to foretell both marriage and pregnancy. One simple method of using stars for divination is to formulate a yes/no question, then go outside on a clear night. Look at the stars, wait about 15 minutes and look again. If the stars seem to glow more brightly the second time, the answer to your question is yes, if there is no change in the intensity of the light, or clouds have blotted out the sky, the answer is no. It can be difficult to judge relative light intensities over a 15-minute period, and in many big cities light pollution makes this method impracticable.

Moon

The moon, with her pale, mysterious light and changing shapes, has played an important part in divination in many cultures, and has a prominent role in both Western and Chinese astrology (Chapters 1 and 2). There are many traditions associated with using the moon to foretell the future; perhaps the simplest concerns predicting your fortune over a lunar month. Wait for the day of the new moon. If it is a clear night, go outside and note where you see the moon. If she is directly before you or to your right, the following lunar month will be filled with good fortune, if she is to your left, or you have to turn round to spot her, the month will not be lucky.

Wind

Wind was once thought to be the breath of deities, or sometimes, demons. It has been used for divination in a variety of ways. The way it blows leaves, dust, smoke and sand have all formed the basis of prophetic divination, as has watching the way it blows across water. Two simple methods of using the wind in prediction are:

- Formulate a yes/no question in the evening. The next day, find out from which direction the wind is blowing – this information can be gleaned from local weather forecasts. A northern or a western wind indicates a negative answer to your question. An eastern or a southern wind indicates a positive answer.
- For practical reasons, this method may not be suitable for all readers. formulate a yes/no question, then light a small, garden bonfire taking all normal safety precautions. Watch the way the wind blows the smoke. If it rises straight up, blows to the south or to the east, the answer is negative. If it hangs heavily around the fire, blows to the north or to the west, a positive answer has been received.

Clouds

Clouds may speak to us in symbols, and to that extent, divination through observing the clouds is similar to divination through dream interpretation – to hone your cloud interpretation skills, try the exercise at the end of Chapter 5. If you really study the clouds, giving them your full concentration, you may see symbolic images in them. Ponder the meanings these images could have for you, and their relation to any problem you are currently trying to resolve, or any decision you are about to take.

Flight of birds

As we noted in the Introduction, using birds for divinatory purposes was common in Roman times, in turn the Romans learned this practice from the much older Etruscan civilisation, centred in what is now Tuscany. The Etruscans believed that birds were messengers of the gods and could fly between the realms of men and gods at will. Hence their importance for divination – they were conduits

between the human and the divine and could reveal divine will concerning the future. Birds were watched for their number, their direction of flight, the patterns made when they settled on the ground, or rose as a flock, their cries, the patterns they made when pecking for food. Certain birds were regarded as fortunate omens (e.g. the eagle), others as unfortunate (e.g. the owl).

You can adapt ancient methods to your own life in the following way. Formulate a yes/no question. Go to a place with plenty of trees and a source of water – perhaps by the lake in a public park. Wait for a bird, or birds, to appear in the sky. If the first birds you see fly from right to left, the answer is no, if from left to right, the answer is yes. If the birds fly directly towards you, this is a lucky portent and your answer is yes. If they fly directly away from you, this is unlucky and your answer is no. If no birds appear, your question is not yet answerable.

Fire

Fire is one of the most awe-inspiring gifts of nature, yet we are not here talking about raging forest fires, or great conflagrations, but about using this enormously powerful force of nature in its domesticated form – the household fire or garden bonfire. If you choose to use these methods, take all normal safety precautions. Many traditions concern fire divination. As an example: a spitting fire is said to indicate coming trouble; if a fire refuses to take, hard work will be required; showers of sparks indicate you are about to receive important news; if the fire blazes up, a stranger is about to come into your life. Fire gazing can also provide information, in a similar manner to scrying (see Chapter 3), or cloud gazing (see above). Do not sit too close to the fire, protect your eyes and do not fire gaze for more than a few minutes.

Plants and trees

Divination and prediction through the observation of oak and mistletoe – the patterns in which they grow and die, and the way in which their leaves rustle in the wind, the shadows they throw in the sun – was common in ancient Celtic cultures. Other cultures used yew trees. Divination with leaves, especially fig leaves, was also

widespread in the past. You can adapt this method in the following way. Find any large leaf. Write a specific question on the leaf, or just a key word identifying some major issue in your life. Place the leaf in a safe place. If it quickly withers and dies, this is not a good omen; if it remains fresh and slowly dries, the prospects are favourable. Divination with flowers has also been common in all parts of the world. The well known method of pulling the petals off a daisy while reciting he (or she) loves me, he loves me not is a form of plant divination. Seeds have also been used in divination, especially in methods employing casting the lots. Dandelion clocks were once used to estimate how long it would be before something came to pass – if the querant blew hard against the seed head and all the seeds flew off, the event would soon occur; if a few seeds remained the event would occur, but not yet; if very many seeds remained, the event would not occur.

Troubleshooting

Some of these methods may seem extremely hit and miss. But our attitude towards them perhaps influences their effectiveness. Today we live out of step with nature, we take the earth for granted and abuse her abundance. We spoil the habitat of birds, we poison water, we pollute the atmosphere, and our artificial lights blot out the light of the stars and moon. It is hardly surprising that we frequently fail to attune ourselves to the energies of natural forces, and thus, hardly surprising that they frequently seem irrelevant or confused.

Limitations

None of these methods can foretell the future with certainty – they suggest possible outcomes and paths. Techniques which yield yes/no answers should not be used as the sole basis for decision taking, but as one source of advice amongst many. If you choose, you can use divination employing natural phenomena as apart of

an overall strategy for decision making, encompassing many different approaches.

SUCCESS STORY

Here is a somewhat ironic success story, of sorts, from the ancient world. The last pagan emperor of Rome, Flavius Claudius Jullianus, (332–6 CE [Common Era]) was served, like many of his predecessors, by Etruscan augers – member of a priesthood whose main function was divination through observing birds. His augurs read the auspices and advised the emperor not to make an attack on the Persians, at that time giving trouble on Rome's eastern borders. Flavius Claudius Jullianus ignored their advice – and died in the ensuing battle. Thus the last pagan emperor perhaps died because he did not trust his pagan augurs.

PRACTICE

It is perfectly feasible for you to devise your own method of divination, based on the phenomena of nature. Walk around your garden or a local park. Do any plants or trees particularly catch your attention? Could you use these in helping you to think through yes/no questions? Perhaps you could watch the way the wind moves their branches, or the shadows they cast, or note which of three buds open first (assign yes to one bud, no to the second, and no answer yet possible to the third – the bud which opens first gives you your answer). Or on a visit to your local zoo or aquarium, does the behaviour of the animals suggest anything to you? Could you use observation of the way they eat their food, or move, or stretch and sleep to answer yes/no questions? Once you are alive to the possibilities of harnessing the power of nature in your decision making, the possibilities are endless.

FURTHER READING

The Art of Divination by Scott Cunningham, published by The Crossing Press, contains much fuller information about using natural phenomena in divination than it is possible to give here, and is highly recommended for further study.

Also, the following books in this series give more detailed information on topics covered in this chapter.

Herbs for Magic and Ritual
The Magic and Mystery of Trees
Paganism
Shamanism
Witchcraft

all by Teresa Moorey

7

WHAT IS NUMEROLOGY?

Numerology assigns numerical values to the letters of the alphabet, according to the schema given below. This practice probably had its origin in ancient Israel, where the letters of the Hebrew alphabet also carried numerical values. As a tool for situational and psychological prediction, numerology reflects our fascination with the power, beauty and mystical significance of numbers. Talk of lucky and unlucky numbers reflects the same sort of fascination.

Schema for translating letters into numbers:								
1	2	3	4	5	6	7	8	9
A	B	C	D	E	U	O	F	I
Q	K	L	M	N	V	Z	P	R
J	T	S			W	G	H	
Y					X			

NB: Different authorities give different schemas, the important point is to be consistent.

Why does numerology work?

By exploring the numerical values hidden in our names, and birth dates, we systematically collect numerical information and, thus, come to a sort of statistical understanding of how our personal tendencies and idiosyncrasies will affect a variety of situations.

How can you use numerology for prediction?

An experienced numerologist would draw on many different numbers, all derived from significant facts about you, to provide you with a tool to aid self-understanding and prediction. Here we will look at only three numbers: your name number, your birth number and your year-cycle number.

Name number

This signifies your current overall direction in life, and your currently guiding personality traits.

To find your name number you need to work with the first name by which you are most commonly known, and your current surname, exclude any middle names. If you are called Charlotte Mary Gray, but

are know to all as Lottie, then work with the name Lottie Gray. You convert your name into a one-digit number, using the letter–number correspondences given in the schema above, and using repeated addition, if necessary. Take Leila Bright as an example.

$$L\ E\ I\ L\ A \quad\quad B\ R\ I\ G\ H\,T=$$
$$3+5+9+3+1 \quad + \quad 2+9+9+7+8+2 = 58$$

Reduce two digit numbers to a one-digit number by repeated addition of the two digits. In this case:

$$5 + 8 = 13$$
$$1 + 3 = 4$$

My name number = 4. For the significance and characteristics of the numbers 1–9, and hence of your own name number, refer to the listing given in this chapter.

Birth number

Your name number can change – this often happens if a women marries and chooses to take her husband's surname, or if people acquire new nicknames or if, for some reason, people change their name by deed-poll or adopt a pseudonym. Thus your name number reflects only *current* situational and psychological factors. Your birth number reflects constant, unchanging themes of your life and destiny. Find it by writing out your birthday – using numbers to represent day, month and year. Then find a one-digit number, by addition as before. Here are a couple of examples for different birthdays.

19 March 1950. This becomes 19 / 3 / 1950, which becomes $1+9+3+1+9+5+0 = 28$, then add $2+8 = 10$, then add $1+0 = 1$, to give the birth number **1**.

3 November 1974. This becomes 3 / 11 / 1974, which becomes $3+1+1+1+9+7+4 = 26$, add $2+6$, to give the birth number **8**.

For the significance and characteristics of the numbers 1–9, and hence of your own birth number, refer to the listing given below.

Year-cycle number

Your year-cycle number, which repeats every nine years and changes every year at your birthday, can reveal your probable fortune in any given year. Find your current year cycle number by writing out the date of your last birthday – using numbers to represent day, month and year. Then find a one-digit number, by addition as before. Here are a couple of examples for 'last birthdays'.

19 March 1997. This becomes 9 / 1 / 1997, which becomes 9+1+1+9+9+7 = 36, then add 3+6 to give the year-cycle number **9**.

22 November 1997. This becomes 22 / 11 / 1997, which becomes 2+2+1+1+1+9+9+7 = 32, add 3+2, to give the year-cycle number **5**.

For the significance and characteristics of the numbers 1–9, and hence of your current year-cycle number, use the listing given below.

Characteristics of the numbers 1–9

Within the limitations of the available space, it is possible to give only minimal information about the characteristics of the numbers 1–9.

1 You are innovative, an initiator, independent and an individualist. Beware selfishness, arrogance, being domineering and inconsiderate. As a year cycle number, a good year to simplify your life, put the past behind you and make a new start.

2 You are gentle, artistic, intuitive and diplomatic. Beware of passivity, complacency, being too easily led. As a year-cycle number, a very good year for your existing partnership, or for forming new bonds of intimacy.

3 An excellent communicator, imaginative, adaptable and popular. Beware of over-exaggeration or even deceitfulness, being showy or conceited. As a year-cycle number, a whirlwind year, with lots of opportunities for new experiences and creative challenges.

4 Reliable, steady, practical and cautious. Beware of over-work, stubbornness, falling into a rut, bottling up your emotions. As a

year-cycle number, a time for investing in a secure future – investment may mean financial or emotional investment.

5 Curious with a constant sense of wonder, you like to learn. Beware of wrapping yourself in layers of mystery, distorting the truth, letting any boredom you feel get the better of you. As a year-cycle number, a year of change, you may feel restless, particularly at work. Change could affect your personal life.

6 You are trustworthy, reliable and a good friend, also artistic. Beware of being taken for granted, or becoming overly domestic. As a year-cycle number, a year of balance and harmony, when home and family assume great importance.

7 You are a deep thinker, creative, intuitive and imaginative. Beware of becoming remote or withdrawn, you need to learn to communicate with your fellow men. As a year cycle number, a good year for study and for developing your mental and spiritual life generally.

8 You are a good leader and a hard worker, good at practical problem solving. Beware of becoming either reckless or ruthless in pursuing your goals, try not to let your organisational skills slide into bossiness. As a year-cycle number, a year to reap the rewards of past hard work, but be on your guard against material failure.

9 You are tolerant and determined, a freedom fighter who wants to change the world. Beware being over-enthusiastic, trying to dominate others and becoming quarrelsome. As a year-cycle number, a year of flux and new opportunities – a good year to start to fight for causes you believe in.

TROUBLESHOOTING

Your name number could mislead if, for instance, other people call you by a nickname of which you are unaware. Perhaps, if you are a teacher, your pupils call you Miss Kipperfeet or Old Cardboard behind your back. Or if you are the boss of a large department, perhaps your juniors have some unflattering name for you. If you are commonly known by a name other than the one you use to find

your name number, influences from the other name are likely to render the analysis of your name number inaccurate.

Your birth number and year-cycle number are not open to this kind of inaccuracy, but you, or your experiences in a given year, could be atypical for all sorts of reasons – education, life experiences, health, etc.

Only nine numbers have numerological significance and there are billions of individuals, hence it is best to interpret the meanings assigned to each number as widely as possible, even symbolically, when considering your own life. Skilled practitioners often use numerology as an adjunct in the consultation of other sorts of oracles. The information given here is necessarily brief and you may find a degree of inaccuracy.

Limitations

Remember, numerology is a kind of statistics; it deals in probability and likelihood, not certainty.

SUCCESS STORY

As we saw above, Leila Bright gives a name number of 4. How do I, Leila Bright, think the sketch of 4 characters is relevant to me? As a freelance working in the book world I need to be careful not to take on more work than I have time for, and I certainly bottle up my emotions. I hope I am reliable, but do not think I am particularly cautious. My birthday is 5 November 1963, which yields a birth number of 8. I do not think I am a typical 8, but perhaps this is just because I am blind to my 8 faults. My year cycle number for 1998 was 6, and it is certainly true that home and family, especially children, played a hugely important part in my life in that year.

PRACTICE

This exercise is designed to set you thinking about the power, beauty and mystery of numbers. Go to your local library, or local bookshop, and see what books are available on popular mathematics. Even if you do not think books such as these would interest you, try to find one which appeals and start reading – you might find you get hooked. Similarly, try to watch television programmes on popular mathematics or listen to radio programmes. Also, start a numbers scrapbook – cut out newspaper articles on any aspect of mathematics, or pictures which incorporate numerals. Perhaps you might find yourself becoming intrigued by such questions as what is a number? Do numbers exist in the world?If so, you might like to try reading any introduction to metaphysics, or even the philosophy of mathemathics.

FURTHER READING

The following books in this series give more detailed information on topics covered in this chapter.

Numerology by Kristyna Arcarti
Numerology and Relationships by John C. Burford
Qabalah by Kate Rheeders

8 PALMISTRY

What is palmistry?

Palmistry, which dates back to at least 1000 BCE and may have originated in India, means divination, including prophetic divination, through interpreting the shape and characteristics of the hands, including patterns made by lines, and other features, particularly on the palms. As with other methods of divination, the power of palmistry lies in showing how you can transform your life to alleviate suffering and achieve inner fulfilment.

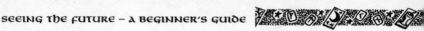

Why does palmistry work?

Your unique character is reflected on your hands. We all make use of this basic insight whenever we use observation of the way strangers use their hands as cues for forming judgements about them – we know that pointing or making a fist while talking can indicate aggression, drumming the fingers suggests boredom or impatience; bitten nails can hint at a nervous disposition; fiddling with rings can show that a person is deep in thought and trying to solve a difficult problem. More systematic study can reveal much about a person's character and hence destiny.

How can you use palmistry for prediction?

Palmistry consists of two parts, the study of:

- the shape of the hand, fingers, joints, nails and thumb
- the lines, markings and other features on the palms and wrists.

In this brief survey, we shall be concerned only with the lines. Both the right hand and the left are studied by palmists, but it is the hand you use to *write* which reveals your future, so that is the hand you should consult while reading this chapter.

The lines

We will look at five major lines represented on most people's palms; physiologically these are caused by the way we flex and tense our hands. Spiritually they map flows of vital energy reflecting an individual's consciousness. A skilled palmist would look at the length, breadth, and quality (broken, appearing to form a chain, etc.) of these lines, and also of others. Here we give only a broad overview of the associations linked to each line. The picture at the beginning of this chapter shows the likely positions of the five lines on your palm. The table in Chapter 1 (pp. 13–14) gives information on planetary associations.

 Life line, ruled by Venus – this line is concerned with health, security, love and money

- **Heart line**, ruled by Jupiter – concerned with sex, emotions and relationships.
- **Head line**, ruled by Mercury- concerned with the mind, communication and education
- **Fate line**, ruled by Saturn – concerned with work, worldly progress and material success
- **Sun line**, ruled by Apollo – concerned with creativity and recognition.

When using palmistry to try to predict timing of future events, it is important to know in which direction each of the lines should be read.

- **Life line** – read downwards towards the wrist.
- **Heart line** – this begins at your little finger and is read across towards your thumb.
- **Head line** – read across from the end nearest your thumb.
- **Fate line and sun line** – these lines are read upwards towards the fingers.

To determine likely timings of events, use a marker pen to divide each line into blocks of seven years. For longer lines this is easy, for shorter lines extend them in your imagination and divide the whole length into blocks of seven, as if the line were longer. The date at which the events or characteristics governed by the line came into effect or ended is given by the date revealed at the actual start or end of the line. You can test the accuracy of your timescale by seeing if important past events in your own life are represented on your palm – for example, is the year you married represented by some feature on your heart, fate or life line? Any unusual looking marking on or around the line could be significant.

The line of fate can be particularly helpful in estimating the timing of major events. This is because it reveals our path through life and our destiny more precisely than the other lines. Lines intersecting with the fate line indicate people or events which are instrumental in our lives.

One important fact to bear in mind is that a short life line does not indicate a short life, and certainly none of us can know the hour of our death. The life line is concerned with life and vitality, not with morbidity.

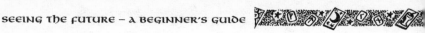

TROUBLESHOOTING

If you want detailed information, consult an experienced palmist. This book gives an introductory sketch only; we do not discuss some of the lesser, but still important lines, (e.g. the intuition line ruled by the moon, and the temper line ruled by Mars). Nor have we looked at any of the markings you might encounter on your palms, nor at how the shape of your hand and fingers might affect a reading.

It can be extremely difficult to learn to decipher the meaning hidden in our hands. Real hands do not look remotely like the neat diagrams given in palmistry books. Real hands have lines missing, double lines, branched or forked lines, intersecting lines, lines which appear to fall in the wrong place, etc. If you are having trouble identifying even the five lines mentioned above, do not become discouraged, rather keep practising and refer to some of the books listed below for more detailed information.

LIMITATIONS

Like the other techniques explored in this book, palmistry is concerned with helping you to increase your self-understanding and to find added meaning in your life. It deals with potential and possible transformation, and cannot anticipate predetermined events. Note that our free will is reflected in our hands – the lines can change quite suddenly as we choose to make changes in our lifestyles, by moving to another country, getting married, changing jobs, having children or whatever.

SUCCESS STORY

James, a book designer considering going freelance, consulted an experienced palmist about the likely success of such a venture. To the palmist the relative positions of his head and life lines indicated spontaneity, and the angle of his head line suggested he was imaginative – spontaneity and imagination would both be key to his success as a freelance. His fate line rose from just inside his life line, showing he has

another requisite quality – self-motivation. His sun line was alternately clearly and poorly defined, indicating a repeating pattern of material success and hardship – something he would have to accept if he left the world of secure employment. The way in which his fate line crossed his heart line indicated he would have continuing fulfilment from his work. His fate line also revealed his current state of confusion about which direction he wanted his professional life to take, and indicated some major event around his thirty-fifth birthday, two years in the future. James' reading brought several difficult issues into focus, but gave no easy answers, underlining the fact that our hands do not tell of a predetermined fate, but reflect our dynamic interaction with our world.

PRACTICE

This exercise will help you to familiarise yourself with the lines of your own hand. Take a fine-tipped felt pen of *washable* ink and draw along each of your major lines, dividing each into blocks of seven. Identify each of the five major lines discussed above. Notice how many other lines there are on your hand and how many other features. Can you see chains in any lines, or stars, or crosses anywhere on your palm? Meanings of all these can be revealed with further study. Where do the lines intersect? Are they long or short, faint or clear? Can you see any patterns on your wrists?

Of necessity, you will have to ink over the lines on your non-writing hand, but remember that when it comes to issues concerned with the future, you will have to look at your *writing* hand.

FURTHER READING

Palmistry for beginners by Kristyna Arcarti, published by Hodder & Stoughton, 1993
Teach Yourself Palmistry by Ray Douglas, published by Hodder & Stoughton, 1998

RUNES

WHAT ARE RUNES?

A rune is any letter of the alphabet used by Northern European peoples from about the third century BCE. Runes were initially formed by modifying Greek or Roman characters to suit carving – all are composed of easily carved straight strokes. In addition to their mundane uses, runes always served as a magical alphabet, enabling communication between the realm of humans, and that of the gods. Runic symbols carried layers of meaning above their ordinary use as part of an alphabet – as if our letter *A* stood for a concept such as *immortality*, and also carried other meanings which had to be understood through intuition and contemplation, which might only

be available to the initiated. Today the divinatory power of the runic symbols can be harnessed to help to resolve past problems and present concerns, as well as hinting at future destiny.

Why do runes work?

If the runes are believed to be a magical set of pictographs representing the forces and objects found in nature, then it is a short step to conclude that by calling on a particular rune, one can interact with and learn from the natural force it represents. Above all, runes are symbols; you can bring the same kind of interpretative skill to bear on runes as you do to the symbols presented in dreams (see Chapter 5).

How can you use runes for prediction?

For divination, the most commonly used form of the runes is the oldest, known as the Elder Futhark. This comprises twenty-four runes, grouped in three sets of eight – Freya's Eight (or *aett*), Hagall's Eight and Tir's Eight. An additional rune, wyrd, is added to the Elder Futhark. Wyrd is a blank runestone. (For meanings associated with the individual runes, see pp. 68–71.)

Runes can be made of almost any material – wood, stone or bone all being common. Some insist that runes should be made of wood from a fruit tree. For the best results, try to make your own runes.

There are various methods of consulting the runes; here we shall be concerned with one – the clockface method – which uses all the runes, and also the three-rune spread, which uses only three runes.

Clockface method

This is a good method to employ at the beginning of a new venture, if you want a quick overview of the coming twelve months. Place all the runes in a pouch and shake it thoroughly. Remove the runes one

at a time and lay them out, as if on a clockface. Place the first two runes at one o'clock, the second two at two o'clock, and so on round to twelve o'clock. Place the twenty-fifth rune in the middle (see below).

Months are represented by their position on the clockface. One o'clock represents the month following the reading, two o'clock represents the month after that. For example, if the reading is in June, one o'clock represents July, two o'clock August, etc. The runes are read as pairs. The twenty-fifth rune, in the centre, indicates the pervading influence over the whole year, and each pair of runes should be read with this in mind. If a rune is inverted (upside down when you pick it out) then its influence is dissipated.

Three-rune spread

This is useful when you want to consult the runes about a specific issue. Formulate your question as clearly as you can, but do not feel constrained to cast it in yes/no form. Place all the runes in their pouch and shake it. Concentrate hard on your question while taking out three runes. Place the runes in a row, from left to right, in the order selected. Traditionally, the first rune is concerned with the underlying cause, or complex of causes, giving rise to the issue

concerning you, the second is concerned with the issue in the here and now, and the third indicates possible future outcomes. If you think of the runes as forming a story with a beginning, a middle and an end, it might make it easier for you to interpret their meaning.

Rune meanings

Note that it is difficult to transliterate the names of the runes into English, so you will see a variety of spellings of rune names. There are also slight variations in the pictographs of the runes.

Feoh – the rune for cattle, metaphorically the rune of material gain, fulfilment and prosperity. It also indicates new beginnings and creative energy. Paired with a love rune, it can indicate a romantic gain or new relationship. If paired with negative runes, it can indicate you should be concentrating on what you already have, not seeking new gains.

Thorn – a vexing thorn, minor problems or petty irritations. Strong links with protection – this is the glyph for the Hammer of the God Thor – and also with luck. It may herald a stroke of good luck, or the end of a run of good luck, depending on other runes in the cast.

Rad – wagon, metaphorically travel and movement. A time of change, when plans should be implemented. Action is indicated – on the domestic or career fronts. Perhaps you will be moving home or offices.

Gyfu – gift; this rune is a great gift in a cast. Note it has no reverse position. Joint ventures and partnerships of all kinds, but especially of the romantic kind, are particularly favoured. It also indicates gifts of all kinds – material and emotional, giving and receiving. A will might be indicated.

Ur – wild ox, metaphorically untamed power, energy and vitality. Often indicates the power or importance of the masculine. Good health is strongly indicated by this rune – emotional, physical and mental. Change and expansion are promised – a good time to make career changes.

Os – Associated with the warrior god Odin, this signifies divine protection and wisdom. It can refer to an older person, mentor or wise counsellor. Intellectual endeavour is encouraged. Communication skills are likely to be enhanced, and inspiration is likely. An exam of some sort may be indicated.

Cen – fire; the domestic hearth. The rune of creativity, important to artists and craftspeople. It can also signify a birth, or the birth of an idea or movement. A rune of hope and inspiration, promising success. Stresses the importance of the home and domestic protection.

Wyn – joy; wyn is an auspicious rune heralding happiness coming into your life. Romantic or marital relationships will be harmonious, health will be good and business ventures will be prosperous. In combination with other runes, it indicates success in the area they govern, for example if it falls with rad, wyn indicates a fulfilling journey.

Hagel – hail. This represents forces outside your control, limitation and delay. A good time to reconsider aims and your direction. Be prepared for the unexpected – a calculated risk could pay off.

Nyd – the counsel of patience. Nyd indicates a time of transition, often difficult, which nevertheless offers opportunity for learning and personal growth. Not a time to accept easy answers; think before acting.

Eoh – the yew tree, metaphorically protection. Adopt a positive attitude and Eoh can help you change potential tragedy into triumph. Focus on the future, make long-term plans, but accept that delay can have a purpose.

Peorth – mystery, hidden things and secrets. Perhaps something hidden for many years is about to come to light – a lost object, or long-suppressed family skeletons. News may come from afar. This is also the rune of unexpected good fortune, perhaps a financial gain or an unexpected gift.

Is – ice, metaphorically a time of freeze in relevant endeavours. Patience and perseverance are needed; this may be a time of isolation or separation. There may be a cooling in relationships – business, marital or romantic.

Ger – harvest, metaphorically the reaping of just rewards for past effort. The culmination of a project is indicated, a good time to make deals or negotiate contracts. Legal help and legal affairs are often indicated.

Eolh – rely on the power of your instinct, intuition and insight. You may even be able to tap psychic powers. A rune denoting friendship and help coming from an unexpected quarter.

Sigel – a rune of victory, health and vitality. Difficulties are easily overcome, enabling you to relax and gather your strength. Embarking on a course of study or vocational training is well favoured, as is travel. You can make effective changes in your life.

Tir – another rune of victory, success against the odds and competition. You are willing to fight for what you believe in, and may be, or become, passionately involved in a political or moral cause. Bold schemes of all sorts are well favoured; you are highly motivated, show strength of mind and singleness of purpose.

Beorc – a fertility rune, signifying new beginnings and growth. It always indicates a birth, but not always a literal one – perhaps the birth of an idea. Beorc can represent your mother or your children and can stand for the domestic hearth – joy is indicated. Marriage is also strongly indicated.

Lagu – another rune of intuition, strongly hinting at psychic powers and mental abilities of all kinds (e.g. enhanced memory). Pay particular attention to dream messages, if lagu appears in a rune cast, particularly if you are female.

Ing – the end of a cycle, or the completion of a major task, possibly a milestone event such as a marriage (the end of your single years) or the birth of your first child (the end of your freedom years). Ing indicates a time of consolidation, a time to reflect, before embarking on the next phase or cycle.

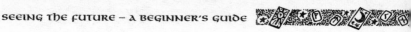

M **Eh** – movement and change, perhaps a house move or an office move. Travel is strongly indicated. Change is usually anticipated and usually for the better. Good judgement and common sense are indicated, but you also need to keep the emotions in balance.

M **Man** – interdependence, of all humankind. A problem can be solved through co-operation. Beware conflicts with authority and do not become so involved in a problem you lose all sense of perspective.

M **Daeg** – increase and growth, promise and fulfilment. Growth is slow and steady, not meteoric. A major life change may be indicated; this may be a situation over which you have no control, in which case you have to make the best of the altered circumstances.

X **Odal** – money, gifts and inherited possessions. If reversed, there will perhaps be conflict over an inheritance, or other argument about money. Land or buildings can also be indicated – property deals are well favoured. Sometimes it signifies meanness, sometimes a hard worker.

Wyrd – the blank rune. The way in which the forces of fate move (or do not move) in our lives. It represents events and influences entirely outside the querant's control. These may produce a dramatic and fundamental change in the querant's life.

TROUBLESHOOTING

If the runes never seem to offer you any intelligible advice, or offer irrelevant or confusing advice, remember that the information given here is brief – further study on the meaning of the runes may clarify matters for you (see Further Reading, at the end of this chapter). Also, bear in mind the constant difficulty of interpreting symbols (see Chapter 5 for more on dream interpretation).

LIMITATIONS

The runes cannot show you what will happen, only offer suggestions about what might happen. They suggest a range of variables, given the way the world is, and you are, now. There are no absolutes. Part of their point is to allow you to take charge of any situation indicated in a runecast and thus *change* the predicted outcome. They do not convey a message about your predetermined fate.

SUCCESS STORY

The other sections of this book all have success stories, but here it seems appropriate to re-tell a story providing a symbolic explanation of how the runes were first revealed, as it emphasises that they act as a means of communication between the everyday world, the world of humans, and another world (or other worlds), of powerful natural forces and, perhaps, of gods. According to Norse mythology, one-eyed Odin, leading warrior god of the Vikings, was the first to discover runes. In an act of sacrifice he hung himself upside down from the mighty Yggdrasil, or World Tree, which forms all the nine worlds of men and spirits, in order to learn the secrets of life and death. His ordeal lasted nine days and nights. During this time, he saw stones carved with the runic symbols, far below him. He seized the stones, contemplated and understood the meaning of the runic symbols and passed on his new-found knowledge to a few human initiates, allowing them to use runes in magic ever since.

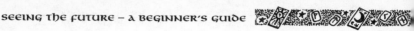

PRACTICE

This exercise asks you to think in depth about the symbolism of the runes. You are going to use the method of the three rune spread, but without formulating any specific question or focusing on any a particular issue. Choose your three runes, then lay them out as indicated above. Tell yourself a story, with a beginning, a middle and an end. The beginning, indicated by the first rune, should be in the past. The middle, indicated by the second rune, should be in the present, and the end, indicate by the third rune, should be in the future. Repeat this story-telling exercise many times, to familiarise yourself with the influence and significance of the runes.

Example

Say you drew gyfu, is, ur. This could refer to a full-time caregiver, who for many years had been willingly offering full, unpaid support on the home front, but who, for the past year, had begun to feel that others were making unjustified demands on her (gyfu). She needs patience and to accept her state of stasis, in the hope that perseverance may lead to the resolution of her problems (is). She has the driving force and the energy to change and expand her role, she has courage and initiative, and will advance her social status – perhaps by starting on a new career, (ur).

FURTHER READING

A Practical Guide to the Runes: their uses in divination and magic by Linda Peschel, published by Lewellyn Publications, is a good source to supplement this chapter.

Also, the following books in this series give more detailed information on topics covered in this chapter.

Runes by Kristyna Arcarti
The Norse Tradition by Pete Jennings

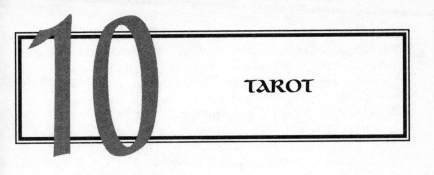

TAROT

· THE SUN ·

What is tarot?

Tarot is a branch of *cartomancy* – the art of reading past, present and future in cards. At its most basic, the tarot is a set of old pictures, set down on paper – the original images are at least medieval, if not older. Most people can learn to read the cards, although this will come more easily to some than to others.

Why does tarot work?

At least two factors need to be borne in mind when trying to explain why the tarot works.

- The general principle of synchronicity, explained in the Introduction. This holds that apparently random events, in this case the order in which cards are drawn, are not really random at all, but are linked to subtle changes in the forces of consciousness and energy pulsing through us and through the universe.
- Your skill in working with and interpreting symbols – another constant theme of this book. Symbols are the language of the tarot; if you need to practise working with symbols, review the text on dream interpretation in Chapter 5 and be sure to work through the exercise given in the practice box.

How can you use tarot for prediction?

To use the tarot, you need a grasp both of the meaning of individual cards and of how they work together in a spread.

The tarot is divided into two parts, the major arcana and the minor arcana. The major arcana is composed of twenty-two numbered picture cards which, apart from the fool, have no equivalent in a standard pack of cards. The minor arcana is composed of fifty-six cards, divided into four suits – swords, wands, cups and pentacles – each suit has cards numbered from one to ten, plus a king, queen, knight and page. The modern deck of playing cards is derived from the minor arcana of the tarot.

Here, we are going to concentrate on coming to understand the meanings contained in the images of the major arcana – which alone bear enough material to set us thinking for a lifetime. A vast number of different packs are available, but beginners are probably best using the IJJ pack, or the Rider-Waite pack. You will need your own pack if you develop a serious interest in the tarot.

It is possible to give only the briefest discussion of the meanings of the cards and, in any case, the tarot has different meanings for different people – that is a large part of its power. When using the cards, remember they all work together in a reading. If cards are inverted, their meaning is generally dissipated (as with runes), or

sometimes even reversed. Using the information supplied here, you will not be in a position to offer readings to other people, rather it will start you on a journey of self-discovery, to be continued through many years of further study.

The major arcana

The following table summarises the meanings of the cards of the major arcana.

Card number	Card name	Meaning
0	The fool	The fool can herald the start of a journey of self-discovery. Think about how you feel about this journey. Expect the unexpected – fresh starts, new horizons, new challenges.
1	The magician	Accept the power of your imagination and all your intellectual skills. Do not be inflexible and do not rely on others to guide you through a problem.
2	The high priestess	A card about the importance of learning, especially through or about women. Inherited knowledge and common sense are part of feminine wisdom, as is intuition.
3	The empress	This card can deal with fertility and creativity. It may herald births or weddings. However, it need not foretell mothering in a literal sense, but the experience of bringing something to fruition.
4	The emperor	Masculine leadership, logic and power – especially worldly power. We must not let emotion or

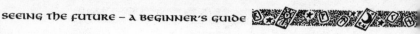

		passion lead us astray, but allow our intelligence and reason full play.
5	The heirophant	Be warned against acting in ways which violate spiritual or moral codes of behaviour – we must act in harmony with the energy of the world. This is the card of spiritual seeking, psychic power, mystery and inner wisdom.
6	The lovers	Choices in relationships, which need to be guided by our inner self but not misled by temptation. Choices might be between a relationship or a career, or between two partners, or between leaving an old relationship or entering a new one, etc.
7	The chariot	Movement, challenge and conquest. Our conquests may not be easy, there could be ordeal and trouble, but we will emerge all the stronger. This is a card of competitiveness.
8	Justice	Balance, moderation and fairness, all with strong legal connotations. It may herald your becoming involved in a legal wrangle, or entering an important contract. There is a need for impartiality and objectivity.
9	The hermit	This card points to the importance of self-denial and reflection. A period of contemplation, possibly solitary contemplation, is called for. Older people are likely to be important at

		this time, and it is a good time for furthering your formal education.
10	Wheel of fortune	Good luck and success, and bad luck and ill fortune. Material desires are important. Also, we must learn to let go of the past in order to progress through life.
11	Strength	Spiritual and bodily strength. Put your plans into action with courage and conviction. The card indicates recovery from illness, so this is a good card to draw if you are sick.
12	The hanged man	Often thought of as a frightening card, the hanged man is about sacrifice and perspective, about suffering, but also about grace. This is a card about expanding our consciousness.
13	Death	This need not be about literal death, but death of an idea, a relationship, etc. People or things may want to hold you back, but you should resist. Something is ending, you need to move on.
14	Temperance	We need to be patient, self-controlled and calm, and to recognise the wisdom of moderation in all things. A card of regeneration, we cannot allow restlessness to waste our energy.
15	The devil	Hidden forces at work, against which we should be prepared. It could be important to disentangle yourself from complex obligations. Be careful how you use your money.

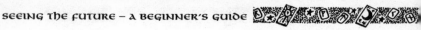

16	The tower	The card shows a falling tower, not a standing one. When buildings fall there is shock and disruption, and people can get hurt. But it is usually possible to rebuild the building, and make it more beautiful and stronger than it was before.
17	The star	Hope. This card heralds improvements, good fortune, good news, rest and relaxation. We should learn to guard against unjustified self doubt and trust our inner strength and wisdom.
18	The moon	Sometimes this card indicates a cross-roads in life. It is often a card heralding uncertainty and emphasising the importance of reflection. We are becoming aware of hidden depths, and need to ponder their meanings.
19	The sun	The life-force of the higher self and of our whole earth. A card of safety after struggle – there is light at the end of the tunnel. In career matters, the sun can herald promotion; in a new marriage it can indicate long-term happiness.
20	Judgement	We may find ourselves rewarded for past actions, alternatively, we may start to act to set right wrongs committed in the past. Things we have suppressed may reassert themselves in our lives; it is a good time to acknowledge mistakes and failures, and to make amends.

| 21 | The world | The summation of all the earlier cards. When we have ended one journey, another must begin. When we feel we have met our targets and achieved our aims, it is time to set new targets and aims. We must always strive after perfection. |

Suggested spreads

I will suggest only two simple spreads; in each case you can use only the cards of the major arcana until you feel ready to undertake further study and introduce cards of the minor arcana, too. The immediate aim is to get comfortable with the stories locked in the major arcana. Shuffle the cards well before starting.

The seven-card spread

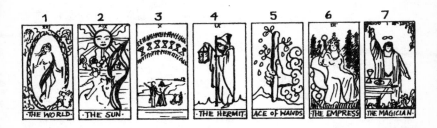

Card 1 = distant past
Card 2 = immediate past
Card 3 = present influences
Card 4 = present obstacles
Card 5 = immediate outlook
Card 6 = future influences
Card 7 = ultimate result.

The ten-card spread

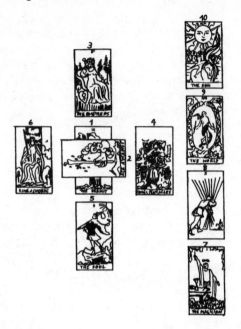

Card 1 = present
Card 2 = immediate obstacles
Card 3 = specific goal
Card 4 = past foundations
Card 5 = past
Card 6 = future
Card 7 = the querant
Card 8 = environmental factors
Card 9 = emotions
Card 10 = result.

You will notice that both these spreads deal with past, present and future. This is because of the impossibility of separating past, present and future in our lives.

Troubleshooting

If the tarot makes no sense to you or appears to give contradictory messages, try to clarify the issue you are addressing, then consult the tarot again – if you are confused in your aims, you are also likely to be confused in your interpretation of the cards. If you still fail to receive meaningful insight, simply trust that as you practise and undertake further study, the tarot will gradually reveal itself to you.

Limitations

You are a free agent. Your tarot cards cannot tell you what is going to happen, only what might happen and how you might handle it, learn from it, avert it, etc. Think of the tarot as a sort of guide to your psyche, as much as a guide to the future.

SUCCESS STORY

Janice was a childless career woman in her late thirties, unmarried, but in a happy, committed relationship. She asked for a reading as part of a sustained attempt to think through how to create new directions in her life. Her reading indeed indicated a period of reflection was going on (the moon), and that decisions had to be made, following a period of patience. Further study was strongly indicated (the hermit). She also drew the devil card, warning her against being tied to someone or something against her will. Janice interpreted this constraining force as her job, and a few months later she and her partner both quit their jobs and decided to spend three months driving across America. On their return, Janice took up a place at her local college, with the ultimate aim of taking a language degree at university.

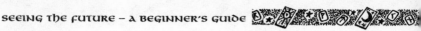

PRACTICE

This is about looking for layers of meaning in the cards of the major arcana. Pick any card and then just indulge in free association of ideas. Look at the card and note anything which pops into your head – do not edit your thoughts. Repeat this exercise as often as you like.

Examples

The hermit: Deserts, old men in deserts, dirty old men in deserts, hardship, sacrifice, craziness, wisdom, sacred wisdom, revelation, belief and disbelief, loneliness, isolation, silence, spiritual quest, doubt, certainty.

The Star: Beauty, energy, explosions, guiding lights, the zodiac, navigation, navigation at sea, light pollution, no stars in cities, the moon, planets, black holes, astronomers, telescopes, music of the spheres, glory of the heavens, mystery, light, mysterious light.

FURTHER READING

Tarot for beginners by Kristyna Arcarti, published by Hodder & Stoughton, 1993
Teach Yourself Tarot by Naomi Ozaniec, published by Hodder & Stoughton, 1998

PART

TWO

Dictionary
of Prophetic
Divination

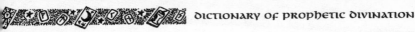

ANIMALS

Many methods of prediction rely on observation of animals. The Azande of Africa observe the way in which termites destroy wood to answer yes/no questions. Many cultures which rely on the sea use patterns left by crabs in the sand for divination. Snakes have been regarded as having divinatory power in cultures as diverse as the ancient Greeks and the Aztecs. Some Native American tribes use mice in prediction and a whole branch of divination is devoted to studying the squeaking of mice. Horses also figure in many methods of divination, ancient Celtic and Germanic peoples both kept sacred horses for divining the future, especially of likely success or failure in battle. Snails are used to determine the possible identity of one's future spouse, by tracing initials in flour or ashes with their slime. Until recently, the Chinese employed a method of divination using turtle shells, a practice also found in modern Africa.

ANIMALS, SACRIFICIAL

Throughout the ancient world, animal sacrifice was common. Members of the relevant priesthood would examine the entrails of the sacrificial animal, especially the liver, looking for favourable, or unfavourable portents – significant signs of something to come.

APOLLO

According to the Greek pantheon, Apollo was the god of prophecy and foresight. A fight with a gigantic serpent, Python, gave him the seat of his oracle at Delphi (see p. 5). Python issued revelations through a fissure in the rock, so that his priestess, the Pythia, could answer querants' questions. After Apollo slew the serpent he took Python's place, and the Pythia henceforth served the god. (*See also* Cassandra).

APPLES

Apples, the peel, pips and stalk, play a significant part in divination concerning love and marriage. If the apple is peeled in an unbroken paring, and this paring is then thrown over the querant's head, it is

supposed to fall in the initials of their future partner. Similarly, if the stalk is twisted once for each letter of the alphabet, the letter at which it breaks is supposed to be significant. If apple pips pop on being tossed into a fire, that is supposed to indicate true love; if they fail to burst, that indicates deception. A year in which there is a bumper crop of apples is said to be a good year for twins. If apple blossom is brought inside a house, that is supposed to foretell sickness.

ARROWS AND AXES

Throughout the world for many centuries, if not millennia, the bow and arrow were essential tools, both for warfare and hunting. It is not surprising that many cultures developed divinatory techniques based on the path taken by arrows in flight, the way in which they landed – sticking straight up out of the ground, leaning at an angle, or falling flat – and the marks they left, or failed to leave, when fired against rocks or wood. Arrows can also be used in a form of casting the lots – arrows are marked or notched, placed in a quiver and selected at random by the querant or candidates for some role. Arrows can also be placed point down in a vessel, their movements used to offer hints about the future. Just as the future was once foretold through observing how arrows landed on the ground, so it was also foretold by observing how a thrown axe, correctly tossed, behaved. Predictions were made from the direction in which the axe handle pointed and the length of time the axe remained standing before falling to the ground.

Ashes

In many parts of England, it was once believed that if one smoothed down the ashes from a fire on New Year's Eve, one would see pictures in the ashes the next morning. These could be used to suggest what the year ahead might hold. A ring would indicate a wedding, a grave a death, a wagon might indicate travel, etc. A snail could also be placed on smoothed ashes and the trails left by its slime used to foretell the future (*see* Animals, above).

ASTROLOGY: WORLD TRADITIONS

This book included discussion of the Western astrological tradition which originated in the ancient near-East, and the Chinese tradition (*see* Chapters 1 and 2). But most, if not all, cultures have evolved means and systems of judging the occult influences of the stars and planets on human affairs. African peoples, Native Australians, Native Americans and the people of the Indian subcontinent all have significant living traditions. Historically, the indigenous people of what is now called Latin America, the Egyptians and many others all had significant traditions.

BIBLE

In distinctly unchristian practices, the Bible was often used as a tool for prophetic divination, sometimes using the methods given under Books, below. Often a key was fastened to the Bible by string. Various methods employing the Bible and keys were devised and used to either identify thieves or future spouses, and also to give answers to yes/no questions. Sometimes specific verses from the Bible were recited as it was consulted as an oracle.

BONES

Many types of bone are, or have been, used in divination. The blade (shoulder) bone from a variety of animals has been particularly widely used. The blade bone is usually marked, often with nine scratches, and then placed under the querant's pillow, in the hope of provoking a dream of their future spouse. The patterns seen in skulls can also be used by the initiated for divinatory purposes. Bones have often been used as lots. The Bantu of South Africa use four bones, representing an old man, a young man, an old woman and a young woman. These are tossed on the ground enabling predictions to be made from the patterns they form. In lot casting, bones may be mixed with shells, stones or other objects.

Books

Books have been used for foretelling the future in at least two ways. A book, any book, was opened at random and the text used to reveal the future. Alternatively, the querant asked a yes/no question to which they knew the answer, then used a pin to select a sentence at random, counted up the number of letters in the sentence and used whether this was odd or even as a means of determining how odd and even were correlated with yes and no. The querant could then use this method to find the answer to problematic questions. (*See also* Bible.)

Buttons

According to folklore, the buttons on a garment can be counted while reciting 'tinker, tailor, soldier, sailor, rich man, poor man, beggar man, thief', to reveal the occupation of a future spouse. There are several variations on this rhyme. The number of buttons can also be used to predict the number of years before marriage, or any other significant event – recite 'this year, next year, sometime, never', to find the likely timing. In each case, buttons can be replaced with fruit stones.

Candles

Candles have been used in a great many ways, by those wishing to foretell the future. The colour of the candle has often been thought significant, with particular colours being associated with particular types of question (e.g. green for money and jobs, pink for friendship, etc). Often candle divination is performed on New Year's Eve to predict the quality of the year ahead. If you wish to try this, light two white candles on New Year's Eve – white is suitable for all types of question. If the candles both burn well with tall, clear flames, this portends a good year, if both splutter and smoke, this suggests ill fortune. If one burns well and the other splutters, or if they both burn in a noncommittal, ordinary sort of way, the year ahead will be much like the last one. If you wish to use candles to answer yes/no questions, get hold of two small candles, assign one to yes, the other to no. Light them both together and see which one burns longest to get your answer.

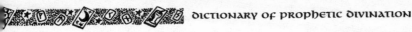

CARD DECKS

The general name for divination using card decks is cartomancy.
Divination with the tarot is a from of cartomancy (*see* Chapter 10).
The standard card deck can also be used.

CASSANDRA

Cassandra was the daughter of King Priam of Troy. She was
endowed with prophecy by Apollo in return for a promise of her love.
When she broke her word, the angry god punished her by decreeing
that her prophecies should always be ignored. She accurately
predicted the fall of Troy to the Greeks, but could not persuade her
kinsmen to believe they were doomed. (*See also* Apollo.)

CHILDREN

In the past divinatory methods were frequently used to help identify
the sex of unborn babies, the future destiny of a newly born child
and the number of children a woman might bear. Many
superstitions surround these questions.

COMET

Comets have, since ancient times been believed to herald important
events, most often death, particularly the death of a monarch, or
disaster such as plague, war, famine or flood. In England, comets
were said to foretell the fall of Harold to William the Conqueror, and
the deaths of King Charles II and Edward VII.

CUCKOO

The direction and place from which you hear the first cuckoo of
spring is said to be significant. If it is from the left, that means ill-
luck for the following year; if from the right, that means good-luck. If
you first hear the bird when standing on grass or green leaves, you
will live to hear cuckoos the following year, if you first hear the
cuckoo when standing on anything other than grass or leaves, your
survival for another year is not so certain.

Destiny

Destiny is a power that foreordains with an unshakeable necessity. This book takes the view that humans act freely, not according to destiny.

Dice

Throwing dice is a form of lot casting (*see* Lot). Three dice can be used for divination. Shake the three dice and cast them on to a suitable surface. Add up the total number shown by the three dice and interpret your score according to the following schema: 3 = pleasant surprises; 4 = unpleasant surprises; 5 = a gain of some kind; 6 = a loss of some kind; 7 = secure finances ahead; 8 = financial difficulties ahead; 9 = a new relationship; 10 = a parting; 11 = a birth, either literal or metaphorical; 12 = a metaphorical death, not a literal one; 13 = sorrow; 14 = joy; 15 = a good time to start new enterprises; 16 = a poor time to start new enterprises; 17 = you need to spend some time at home; 18 = travel and adventure, including spiritual travel and adventure. Different authorities give different suggestions for the way in which these numbers are correlated with the future, so experiment until a secure schema emerges for you.

Eggs

Many divinatory traditions have grown up around eggs. A double-yolked egg is said to presage either a death or a wedding. Breaking eggs accidentally is supposed to presage breaking an arm or a leg. The shapes formed by an egg white after it has been tipped into water are supposed to provide guidance to future events – particularly the occupation of a future spouse. (*See also* Lead and Wax.)

Fates, the

According to Greek and Roman mythology the fates were three goddesses who spun out a child's destiny at birth. One goddess, Clotho, spun out the thread of life, another, Lacheis, measured it and the third, Atropos, cut it.

Fish

The way captured fish swim in tanks can be used as a basis for prediction, as can the types of fish in any given catch. Using fish for divination is common amongst peoples who live by the sea.

Food

Food plays a prominent role in divinatory practices from many cultures. Originally the connection between food and divination probably arose because priests and priestesses interpreted food offerings left for the gods, including the products of animal sacrifice, as an aid to prediction of the future. As well as meat, fish and fowl, nuts, grains and seeds of all types, vegetables and even cheese can be used for divination. Often such divination uses an element of lot casting. (*See* Lot).

Fortune cookie

The modern fortune cookie can perhaps be regarded as a distant descendant of an ancient practice which may have been under the patronage of Apollo. In ancient times, brief outlines of possible futures were written on slips of paper which were then rolled, or baked, in flour balls. The balls were then stirred together and one was selected. (*See also* Written response.)

Geomancy

Geomancy, one of the simplest ways of consulting the hidden forces of nature, is based on interpreting apparently random patterns made in or on the earth. It possibly originated in the deserts of North Africa and may at some time have influenced the development of the I Ching. The method of producing gemoantic figures has varied over time and place. (*See also* Sand reading.)

Graphology

In dream interpretation the products of the mind are studied, in graphology, the products of the hand are studied – namely handwriting. A skilled graphologist will use all aspects of

handwriting, size of letters, spacing of words, degree of angularity in letter formation, general style, beginnings and endings of words, the way individual letters are formed, etc., to come to a detailed analysis of a client's personality and possible future.

Hair

Many superstitions are associated with human hair, and it has often been used in divination – especially to find the identity of a lover, or to predict, from its degree of curliness, how many love affairs a person will have, and even to indicate whether or not a person will marry at all. The way hair burns when thrown into a fire was once believed to indicate the likely length of life remaining to the person from whose head it was pulled.

Ice and icicles

During a cold winter in which icicles form on the overhang of a roof, it is possible to use the way in which they melt for prediction. Two icicles can be used to answer yes/no questions – assign yes to one and no to the other; the icicle which remains in place the longest gives your answer. If you see a group of icicles, assign a specific possible answer to your question to each icicle, again the one remaining in place longest gives your answer. In the summer, or if you live in a place where icicles are rare, you can use ordinary ice-cubes from the freezer in a similar way. If you have only two ice cubes, assign yes to one, no to the other. If you have several ice-cubes assign a given possible answer to your question to each one. Place your ice-cubes somewhere reasonably warm. Your answer is given by the ice cube which melts and disappears the slowest.

Jewellery

Earrings can be used to give answers to yes/no questions. Take two slips of paper, write yes on one, no on the other. Take a pair of earrings and attach the yes slip to one, the no slip to the other. Place both earrings in a cloth bag. Ask your question and pull one out. The slip of paper attached to it gives your answer. Alternatively,

write several possible outcomes on several slips of paper and attach them at intervals along a necklace. Close your eyes, pull the necklace through your fingers and select one slip, apparently at random. This will hint at the decision you might now take. Any type of jewellery is suitable for these methods, including inexpensive fashion jewellery. (*See also* Written response.)

KNIVES

Knife spinning has often been used to ascertain whether a future spouse would be light-haired or dark-haired. This can be adapted to answer any yes/no question. Ask a question to which you know the answer. Then spin a knife to discover whether it stops with the blade or the handle pointing towards you. This will determine the yes/no response. (**NB**: Some traditions count spinning a knife in front of you as ill luck.) A knife accidentally knocked from a table is said to presage the arrival of strangers – the size of the knife is even said to predict the height of the new arrivals; a long knife means they will be tall, a short knife means they will be short. To find a knife lying in the road indicates ill fortune.

Lead and wax

Either lead or wax can be melted and poured into cold water. The shapes these substances form as they harden can be used as omens of the future. Lead can also be used in this way to divine the cause of sickness. (*See also* eggs.)

Leaves

Leaves can be used to predict the outcome of a courtship. There are several variations on this theme, most involving scratching the initials of a loved one on a leaf, then secreting it about one's person for a day. If the initials remain clear, the courtship will progress favourably, if not it is doomed. Laurel leaves were often used in this way. Ivy leaves placed in water on New Year's Eve are said to indicate by their condition after one week the quality of the coming year. *See* chapter 7 for more on divination with plants.

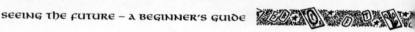

LOT

A lot is (a) one of a set of objects used to secure an apparently random result in dividing goods, selecting officials, etc. (b) what falls to a person by this method of deciding, (c) a person's destiny or fortune. Many methods of prediction rely on casting the lots. The success of these methods can perhaps be explained by referring to the forces of synchronicity (*see* Introduction).

LOVE AND MARRIAGE

In the past, divinatory methods were frequently used to help in matters of love, chiefly to identify a future spouse and to discover whether a lover was true, or deceitful. Drawing lots to find a Valentine was a common practice until recent times in many parts of England. The timing and success of any marriage were also often prescribed.

MAH JONG

Mah jong is the Chinese equivalent of the tarot. A mah jong set consists of a box containing 144 tiles inscribed with Chinese characters. The tiles are divided into four 'packs', each containing thirty-four tiles. The four packs can themselves be sub-divided into: three suits, bamboo, circles and numbers, each containing nine tiles; four directions – north, south, east, west; three colours – red, green and white. In addition, there are eight guardian cards – plum, orchid, chrysanthemum, bamboo, fisherman, woodcutter, farmer, scholar. Like the tarot, mah jong is suffused with astrological and ritual symbolism. It can be used for prediction and divination in ways similar to the tarot, involving apparently random selection of tiles, each of which has a particular significance capable of interpretation by those who have studied the system.

MANTIC ARTS

Mantic, which comes from the Greek word for *prophet*, simply means *of divination*; – *mancy* is very often used as a suffix to indicate a branch of divination e.g. *bibliomancy* means divination

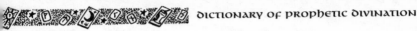

with books (*biblia* is Greek for books), *lithomancy* means divination with stones, (*lithos* is Greek for stone), *cartomancy* means divination with cards (*carte* is French for card).

MARRIAGE

In the past, divinatory methods were frequently used to help identify both the identity of a future spouse and the timing and success of any marriage.

MERLIN

Merlin, a central figure in Celtic mythology, guided his king, Arthur, with wisdom and foresight. Arthur, son of King Uther Pendragon, was conceived out of wedlock and brought up by Merlin. When Uther Pendragon died, Merlin was consulted about who should next become king. He told the knights to select whoever could pull a sword from a stone which had mysteriously appeared in London. Arthur achieved this feat when none other could and attained his destiny. Only with Merlin's aid was the young king able to bring peace to Britain. Merlin made a great many prophecies which were collected in the middle of the twelfth century by Geoffrey of Monmouth and which continue to intrigue scholars today.

MILLENARIAN PROPHECIES

Periods of 1,000 years have always provoked interest and excitement. This is the period predicted for Christ's reign, in person, on earth. Most millenarian prophecies forecast doom and disaster, even Armageddon – supreme conflict between nations. A number of Nostradamus' prophecies are said to concern the millennium – (*see* Nostradamus).

MIRRORS

Mirrors reveal to us things which cannot be seen in any other way. A mirror remains flat, yet it can seem to contain a whole three dimensional scene. Mirror images are the reverse of what we see with our eyes. For all these reasons, mirrors have played a

prominent part in divination through the ages and, in the past, complex rituals grew up around their manufacture and use (glass mirrors were not introduced until comparatively late). Techniques involving the use of mirrors can be similar to those described in the discussion of scrying (see Chapter 3). Mirrors can be used to identify a future spouse, or predict the course of a disease as well as to answer more general questions.

Nostradamus

Nostradamus (1503–66) was a French seer who could apparently produce a state of consciousness in which he could see into the future (*see* Prophets and prophecy). In 1555, when he was 52, Nostradamus published his first Almanac. His prophecies made him famous. Some of his predictions were very precise, giving exact dates for events, some can be extremely cryptic and require detailed study. Amongst other things, Nostradamus is credited with prophesying both the Great Fire of London (1666) and the outbreak of the Second World War (1939).

Oil

Divination using oil dates back at least to ancient Babylon, where the priesthood devoted much time and effort to divination. In the modern world, olive oil can be poured into water and the way in which it floats on the surface interpreted for omens of the future, or motor oil can be poured into puddles (not very environmentally friendly).

Omen/Ominous

An omen is an occurrence or object supposedly portending good or evil. It can also mean to foreshow, or give presage of – *ill-omened*, etc. Bad omens seem to have outweighed good omens in the collective consciousness, hence the word *ominous*, which on the face of it is neutral between good and bad omens, nearly always means *of evil omen*.

ORACLE

In the context of a general discussion of prediction, *oracle* means a person or thing regarded as serving as an infallible, though mysterious, guide to the future. As the variety of entries in this dictionary shows, almost anything is capable of being regarded as an oracle. (*See also* Portent.)

ORACLES: WORLD TRADITIONS

Most, if not all, cultures have evolved means of consulting oracles. African peoples, Native Australians, Native Americans and the people of the Indian subcontinent include those who still have significant living traditions. Historically, the indigenous people of what is now called Latin America, the Egyptians, the Greeks and the Celts all had significant traditions, as did many other peoples. Oracles were usually, but not exclusively, found in the natural world (*see* Chapter 6, Natural phenomena).

PALMISTRY: CHINESE

Chinese palmistry takes a different approach from Western palmistry. The Chinese do not examine the lines of the hand, rather they divide the palm into different areas, each of which represents a different area of life (family, money, etc.). Palmists look for marks resembling Chinese writing characters and interpret their meaning according to whereabouts they lie on the palm.

PHYSIOGNOMY

Physiognomy is the art of judging character from the features or form of a person's body or face – phrenology, the study of the conformation of the skull as a guide to mental faculties, and palmistry are both forms of physiognomy. Many bodily features can be used for divination. A whole web of lore has grown up around moles, warts and other lesions. On a woman, the number of moles can be taken to suggest either the number of husbands, or the number of children she might have. Moles on the back of the neck

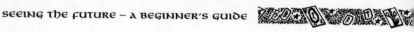

might indicate future criminality, moles on the back likely wealth, etc. Marks in the eye, or on nails, might similarly be used for divination. Patterns of hair growth could also be used.

PLACENTA

In many cultures, examination of the placenta (afterbirth) or burning it after a baby was born were used as an aid to prediction, usually either as a gauge to the likely lifespan of the newborn, or as a means of predicting how many children the mother would eventually have. In the latter case, the placenta was burned and the number of pops it made taken to equal the number of children.

PORTEND/PORTENT

To portend is to foreshadow or to give a warning of. A *portent* is a significant sign of something to come. (*See also* Omen/ominous.)

PROPHETS AND PROPHECY

In non-religious contexts, a prophet is one who has the ability to enter an altered state of consciousness and foretell events directly, through pure psychism, without the need to use formal methods of prophetic divination. A prophecy is a prophetic utterance, foretelling a future event. (*See also* Cassandra, Nostradamus, Merlin) (**NB**: Cassandra was a prophetess in a religious sense, i.e. an inspired revealer of divine will.

QUILTS

In America, the creation of patchwork quilts has reached an art form. Contemplation of hand-crafted quilts lovingly created with passion and flair, especially those of abstract design, can be used to stimulate the conscious mind to recognise symbolic images produced by the subconscious mind, much in the manner of cloud gazing or fire gazing (*see* Chapter 6). Mass-produced quilts will not have the same effect.

RINGS

Rings, particularly wedding rings, are often used to make pendulums for dowsing (*see* Chapter 4). In a variation on this, suspend your chosen ring in an empty glass by means of a cotton thread or a length of wool – do not use synthetic fibre. Ask a question to which you know the answer. Whether the ring knocks against the side only once, or more than once gives you your yes/no answer. Repeat with another question to which you know the answer, to check you have correctly identified the correlation between yes and no, and the number of knockings (one or many). When asking questions to which you do not know the answer, if the ring does not knock against the side, no answer is yet possible.

ROMANY PEOPLE

The Romanies are the gypsy people of Europe. They speak their own language (Romanes) and have a distinct and highly sophisticated culture. Romany people are often especially gifted with psychic skills and many supplement their livelihoods by offering psychic readings of various kinds to the general public.

SAND

Many desert dwelling people use sand as part of their rituals for making prophecies – random patterns left in the sand and the way they intersected with animal tracks were interpreted by the wise as portents of the future (*see* Geomancy). You can adapt ancient methods to use at home in the following way. Fill a tray with sand and use a ruler to level the surface. Then use your fingers to make patterns in the sand – try not to use your conscious mind to direct the patterns you are making – perhaps close your eyes and let your hands roam freely over the sand. When you have finished, contemplate the sand tray and let the undulations you have created suggest images to you, which you can interpret as symbols, using the same skills you use in dream interpretation. (*See* Chapter 5) Symbols that appear on the left of the tray are connected with the

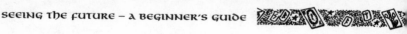

past, those on the right with the future. As a general rule of thumb, symbols that fall closest to where you sat as you made the marks in the sand affect you personally, those that are further away affect people around you.

Shoes

Until recently it was common in England for people to throw shoes over the beams of a house, or into or out of the front door, and then interpret the position and direction of how the shoes fell for clues as to whether they should move into the house, or, if they were already living there, whether they should stay or move on. Perhaps those looking for a new house could use this technique as an aid in decision making – although it might produce some raised eyebrows from estate agents!

Sneezing

The use of sneezing for divination was common in the ancient world. Even recently, the number of sneezes in a row was often considered significant and there are several variations on the following rhyme: 'Once a wish, twice a kiss, three times a letter, four times something better'. The direction of a sneeze – to the right (lucky), left (unfortunate) or directly in front (good news coming) was also thought to be significant. Sneezing and time of day were also often linked. Sneezing before breakfast, or before putting on one's shoes in the morning, and sneezing after the lamps were lighted in the evening, were both interpreted in a variety of ways.

Tea Leaves and Coffee Grinds

Reading the tea leaves, or tasseography, is an ancient art. Select a large-leafed loose tea (not the tea from tea bags) and a tea cup with a large mouth and gently sloping sides. Make your cup of tea without straining the leaves and drink most of it, leaving enough liquid at the bottom to swirl the leaves. Hold the nearly empty cup in your right hand (some authorities say left, but in general the right represents good fortune, the left ill fortune, so it seems safest to use your right hand) and swirl it three times in a clockwise direction.

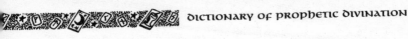

Then invert it over a saucer and allow it to drain. Once the liquid has drained away, you are ready to start reading the leaves. The leaves form symbols. Those closest to the rim of the cup represent the present, those closer to the bottom represent the future. Leaf symbols on the bottom of the cup represent the distant future. Leaf symbols falling close to the handle of the cup represent things, people and events which will affect you personally, those further from the handle will affect those around you. Interpret the leaf symbols using the same skills you drew on for dream interpretation (*see* Chapter 5). Coffee grinds can be used instead of tea leaves and, in Roman times, it was common to use the residue left at the bottom of a goblet of wine.

Tickets, Numbered

Numbered tickets, such as bus tickets, can be used for prophetic divination, sometimes in conjunction with the rhyme: 'One for sorrow, two for joy, three for a girl, four for a boy, five for silver, six for gold, seven for a secret never to be told, eight for a wish and nine for a kiss'. If the last number on a ticket is seven, or if the sum of the numbers is twenty-one, then that is considered to be a lucky portent.

Urine

Throughout history, urine has been considered to have special powers. In the ancient world there was a general fear that urinating inconsiderately might offend the deities and, later, urine was often used in the detection of supposed witches. In some parts of Ireland it was, until recently, believed that if bubbles formed on one's urine, that was a sure sign of financial happiness ahead. Of course, it is entirely accepted and standard medical practice for doctors to use urine in making all sorts of predictions about a person's health.

Virgin

According to some traditions, virgins, of either sex, are supposed to be particularly skilled at divination. Meeting a virgin first thing in the morning used to be thought, variously, to herald a well-favoured or an ill-favoured day, but was certainly thought to be significant.

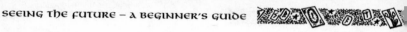

Wheels

The wheel is a powerful symbol for change, and a wheel of fortune is one on which fortune is depicted as turning. Gambling is a basic form of prediction and wheels play a prominent part in many forms of gambling, including roulette and many lottery games. Lotteries also include elements of casting the lots (*see also* Lot).

WRITTEN RESPONSE

Many forms of divination involve writing several possible answers to a question on suitable items – bones, leaves, slips of paper, stones, etc. Then (a) using various methods of eliminating all but one, (b) casting the items to find the favoured answer or (c) otherwise finding the favoured answer. A simple method you can use at home is to write seven possible answers to a given question on slips of paper. Screw them up so it is impossible to read what you have written and place then all in a bowl. Remove one slip each day over a one week period. The final slip remaining gives your answer. But remember that this method, and others like it, though more flexible than methods which simply give a yes/no answer, is limited to the number of possible answers to a question that you manage to think up. Other methods of divination might provide greater scope for your decision making.

FURTHER READING

A *Dictionary of Superstitions*, Edited by Iona Opie and Moira Tatem, published by Oxford University Press, is excellent on English superstitions.

The Art of Divination by Scott Cunningham, published by The Crossing Press, is good on divination using natural phenomena and on more obscure forms of divination. It includes a dictionary of divinatory techniques listed under their technical names, using the suffix -mancy.

The Mammoth Book of Fortune Telling by Celestine, published by Carroll & Graff is good on geomancy, mah jong and Chinese palmistry, amongst other techniques.

The Psychic Workbook by Craig and Jane Hamilton-Parker, published by Vermillion, is a good all-round introduction and is especially good on sand reading and reading tea leaves.

Any good encyclopaedia of mythology will provide background information on aspects of oracles, prophets and prophecies. *The Encyclopaedia of Mythology* by Arthur Cotterell, published by Smithmark, includes discussion of Classical, Celtic and Norse mythology.

Mind and Magic, an illustrated Encyclopedia of the unexplained by Frances X. King, published by Dorling Kindersley, has a section on the future foreseen.

Other titles in this series

To order this series

All books in this series are available from bookshops or, in case of difficulty, can be ordered direct from the publisher. Prices and availability subject to change without notice. Send your order with your name and address to : Hodder & Stoughton Ltd, Cash Sales Department, Bookpoint, 39 Milton Park, Abingdon, OXON, OX14 4TD, UK. If you have a credit card you may order by telephone – 01235 831700.

For sales in the following countries please contact:
UNITED STATES: Trafalgar Square (Vermont), Tel: 800 423 4525 (toll-free)
CANADA: General Publishing (Ontario), Tel: 445 3333
AUSTRALIA: Hodder & Stoughton (Sydney), Tel: 02 638 5299